Praises for

Cue Cards for Men

Boy, where was this book in 1983 before I got married? Although, if she'd read it my wife would've made a better choice also.
--**Robert Wuhl,** *Emmy Award winning Actor, comedian, writer*

***

For a lot of men, the last thing they want to do is see a therapist. It's a stereotype that often rings true. I'm a psychologist myself, and I can barely imagine going to see one of us. *Cue Cards for Men* will help you with the women in your life so that maybe you won't find yourself sitting through hours of therapy.
--**Dr. Brian King**, author of *The Art of Taking It Easy* and *The Laughing Cure*

***

Cue Cards for Men is the perfect read for men seeking a little help in their relationship. From dating to marriage to fatherhood, no stone is left unturned. Good, quick advice that's easy to put to use immediately.
--**Terri Orbuch, Ph.D.**, (aka, The Love Doctor®), author of *5 Simple Steps to Take Your Marriage From Good to Great*, and Distinguished Professor at Oakland University

Cue Cards for Men

A Man's Guide to Love and Life

Written by:

Christina Steinorth-Powell, LMFT

Published by KHARIS PUBLISHING, imprint of KHARIS MEDIA LLC.

Copyright © 2021 Christina Steinorth-Powell, LMFT

ISBN-13: 978-1-63746-077-1
ISBN-10: 1-63746-077-5

Library of Congress Control Number: 2021946842

All KHARIS PUBLISHING products are available at special quantity discounts for bulk purchase for sales promotions, premiums, fund-raising, and educational needs. For details, contact:

Kharis Media LLC
Tel: 1-479-599-8657
support@kharispublishing.com
www.kharispublishing.com

To my one true love, Rusty

You are my happiest smile, my most genuine laugh, and my deepest thought. Every day you inspire me to be my best self. I don't know what I would do without you. You are simply the most lovely, divine man I have ever known. I have loved you and will forever love you hopelessly and deeply. You will never fully understand the place you hold in my heart. Thank you, sweet man, for being who you are, accepting me for who I am, and sharing this one life we have on this Earth.

I love you.

TABLE OF CONTENTS

Introduction ix

1 Chapter One: Cue Cards for Meeting Women 1

2 Chapter Two: Cue Cards for Dating 13

3 Chapter Three: Cue Cards for your Engagement and Wedding 31

4 Chapter Four: Cue Cards for Marriage and Fatherhood 41

5 Chapter Five: Cue Cards for Sex 57

6 Chapter Six: Cue Cards for your Health 63

7 Chapter Seven: Cue Cards for Divorce 73

A Closing Note 87

Resources 89

Introduction

I was on a flight coming back from Los Angeles a couple of weeks ago, and a nice- looking man in his early 30's sat down next to me. As people were boarding the plane, he noticed that a woman was having difficulty placing her luggage in the overhead bin. He got up to help her and asked, "Can I help you with that?" She more than welcomed his assistance. As he sat back down next to me, he said ,"It's tough to be a guy these days." "Why's that?" I asked. He responded, "Well she was open to my help, but just a few minutes ago in the airport, I held the door open for another woman and she told me *I can get the door myself—I don't need your help*." He explained that it wasn't the first time that a woman seemed put off by his offer of assistance. He then told me of a first date he had where he went to open the car door for his date, and she became so angry with him that the date was over before it even began. "She thought I was sexist, hated women...it was something else.... it's tough now...I don't know what I'm supposed to do." We talked about this—the plight of many men these days—for the next couple of hours. It was an interesting conversation. I thought about him the next few days and decided to jump online to see if there were any articles written that addressed his issues. There were very few. It almost felt like *we're not supposed to talk about this*—that's how sparse it was when it came to finding any guidance for this place we are at today with men and women.

What I found is that in the few instances where there seemed to be advice for men and their relationships with women, is that a lot of what's out there is written by *men*. Don't get me wrong; there's nothing wrong with men giving advice to other men. But I think when it comes to men interacting with women, wouldn't you be better served if you listened to how a woman suggested you do it? After all, as a woman, and as a woman who is a counselor for other women in relationships with men, wouldn't I be able to tell you what women want from their men better than a man would?

Before you start to think that I'm going to be advising and lecturing you about how to show your respect for us, not open doors for us or, on the other end, do crafts, cook or go shopping with us, I want to make it clear: I won't. I think that's an awful way to approach advice. I did not write this book to emasculate you. I don't want you to scrapbook, and I don't want you to go shoe shopping. There are very few women who really want that type of interaction with you either. On the flip side, personally, I *want* you to open the door for me and flirt with me a little bit—believe me, I won't be insulted. And you know what? Many other women won't be either. I think one of the greatest things that keeps men and women attracted to one another is that we are in fact *different*. I also think one of the things that drives a man away from a woman is when he feels emasculated in a relationship--who needs that? You don't, I don't, and no woman I've ever talked to does either. Generally speaking, if a woman is in a relationship with you, she would like you to stay around and be happy. When I work with couples who have problems in their relationships, I stress to women that men are more attracted to *us* when we let them be who they're supposed to be, and I also tell them that we'll be more attracted to our men when they're comfortable and confident with who *they* are.

That said, if you're the type of guy who seems to have problems with women, then this is the book for you.

Women aren't that difficult to understand, nor are they that difficult to attract. This book will help you improve your odds at getting more dates and, once you're in a relationship, it will help you keep that relationship going. If you're in a relationship and it hits a rough spot, this book will help you with that, too. I encourage you to use this book like an encyclopedia for the different stages of your love life—from meeting women, to dating them, to marrying them. (For good measure, I've included a chapter on how to be a great Dad and also how to take care of your health—because let's face it, without your health, you won't be able to do much else.) If you're a man who completely stumbles when it comes to all things "women," start with Chapter One and read this book from cover to cover. If you're a man who only seems to have difficulty dating women, turn to Chapter Two. If you're a guy who is getting married, check out Chapter Four. If you've been married and are now facing a divorce, let Chapter Seven help you. Problems in the sex department? Check out Chapter Five. I think you get the idea. You will never have to read this book from cover to cover to get something out of it--just skip to the chapter that you need. Save this book though, because as you progress through your relationships, you never know when you might need a quick shot in the arm, so to speak, to get you back on track. A few Cue Cards here, a few Cue Cards there, and your relationship should be back to where it needs to be.

I wish you much success and happiness with every woman you ever know.

With love,

Christina

Chapter One

Cue Cards for Meeting Women

Did you know that there are roughly 86 men for every 100 women in the United States? Of course, there's some variance to this statistic depending on where you live but, on average, there are usually more women around then men. Given this fact, your chances for meeting women are already statistically stacked in your favor. However, if meeting women was purely a numbers game, there would be very few men trying to figure out how to meet women, and you probably wouldn't be reading this chapter of my book. Since you *are* reading this section, this probably means you'd like to meet more women than you're meeting now.

Have you seen how some men seem to have no difficulty at all meeting women? Why do you think that is? I can tell you that they're probably *not* any better looking, wealthier, or any more intelligent than you are--but they probably possess a few skills you don't. Can you learn or improve your skills to meet more women? Of course, you can. Let the Cue Cards below will help you with this.

Setting the Stage

Improve your odds at meeting women by working on yourself first.

Cue Card: Make a good first impression.

A woman's first impression of you is extremely important, because this is when she decides if she would consider dating you. The good news is that studies suggest that women will give you about an hour to make a first impression (as opposed to the fifteen minutes men usually give women to make a first impression). Here are the cold hard facts: women will base 55% of their initial impression on your appearance and body language, 38% on your style of speaking, and 7% on what you actually say. Therefore, looking good, not acting like a fool, and saying something half-way intelligent and witty will go a long way.

Here are two of the best opening lines I've heard over the years--feel free to use them or, better yet, use them as good examples and create your own:

You look like someone I should get to know.

What I liked so much about this line is that it was complimentary and assertive without being obnoxious.

Another great, although somewhat campy line:

Have we met before?

To which I answered, "No, I don't think so."

His response:

I guess it must have been in my dreams.

As I mentioned, it was campy, but in some cases campy is okay. His line was cute and unique--it showed me that this man had a sense of humor. In general, women like men who are funny and unique--and we also like opening lines that don't focus on our physical appearance.

Cue Card: Be someone women want to meet.

This is probably one of the most important Cue Cards for meeting women. Men on the whole have a great deal more confidence than women, and while it's an admirable trait to be so confident, try to take a step back and look at yourself in a realistic light. Are you the type of man that the type of woman you're looking for would actually want to meet?

Confidence is sexy; arrogance isn't. Have a job. Take care of your appearance. Many men will say that they don't want a woman who is only interested in them for their money, but if you are chronically unemployed or underemployed and looking for a woman to just "love you for who you are and not your wallet," you are really no different than the type of woman many men complain about. I'm not saying you need to make as much money as the woman you are interested in is making, but you should at least be able to contribute from time-to-time with expenses. Women tend to find drive and ambition in men an attractive attribute. If you're unemployed or underemployed, women see this as a lack of ambition and drive. Become more attractive by being employed to the best of your potential.

Cue Card: Have good social skills.

Women are attracted to guys who have good social skills, because we know we will never have to be embarrassed about your behavior. The other reason we value this so much is because when you're skilled socially, you make *us* look better. Good social skills include knowing how to properly use a fork and knife (fingers should *not* be something that ever help you put food on your fork or spoon), and the ability to make small talk. It's also important to know what you can say and to whom, when to stay quiet, and how to dress for an occasion.

If you don't have good social skills, the good news is that they can be learned. You'll have to practice them so they don't look forced, but it will be one of the best investments of time and effort you can make for yourself--not only for attracting women, but you will also find these skills will help

3

your career too. If you're in line for a promotion, supervisors will not only pay attention to how well you do your job, they'll be looking at your social skills too. It's the same reason women value good social skills: when you have them, you make a company look better, and they know they'll be able to trust you to always be a good representative for them.

Cue Card: Make eye contact when you're speaking with someone.

In Western cultures, making eye contact with the person you are speaking with is seen as polite. When you make and maintain eye contact with a person, you indicate to them that you are interested in what they have to say. Have you ever tried talking with someone who is watching television or looking at some type of electronic device rather than you? If so, it wouldn't surprise me if you felt that person was distracted. While it's possible they heard every word you said—after all, some people are great at multitasking—it's more likely you felt they weren't very interested in what you had to say. Making eye contact helps you establish a rapport with the person who is speaking to you. Keep in mind, however, that it's important to be culturally sensitive as well. In some countries, *not* making eye contact actually shows respect. (In short: know your audience.)

When you make eye contact with someone, be careful not to cross the line into staring, which tends to make the person you're talking to uncomfortable. If you have fallen out of the habit of making eye contact (which many people have), try practicing it in a mirror while you maintain a pleasant facial expression. Continued practice with this exercise will help you improve this skill.

Cue Card: Recognize and respect the personal space of others.

One of the most important things you can do when you meet a woman today is to respect her personal space. Many people greet and part from each other with some type of physical gesture, be it a hug, kiss, or handshake, but I strongly advise you not to make any type of physical gesture toward a woman until you get a sense of how it will be received. Each individual—men and women alike--has a personal space, an area they want to maintain around their body to feel comfortable when having a conversation. There is no right or wrong distance, and the person you are conversing with will most likely stand as close to you as they feel comfortable doing. Strive to be sensitive to her personal space during greetings and partings, as well as during conversations.

I'm 100% certain through your own experiences that you are aware that some women are more receptive to physical touch than others, so it's useful to recognize how much touch a woman you are trying to connect to feels comfortable with. It is completely possible to have a great first conversation with a woman and then end with an extremely awkward moment when you bear-hug her and she stiffens up like a board, and you find that you leave her feeling like you completely trampled over her personal space. When in doubt, keep your hands and body to yourself.

Cue Card: Think before you ink.

Unless you've already been married for thirty years to the same person, it's usually not a good idea to get a tattoo of a woman's name placed anywhere on your body. I once worked with a couple who came in weekly for counseling. One day over the summer, the husband wore shorts and I couldn't help but notice the large amount of indistinguishable ink he had on his ankle. "What's that?" I asked. He explained that when he was nineteen, his first wife told him that if he really loved her, he would get her name tattooed on his ankle. (Yes, I know--nothing shows love more than your name on someone's ankle). I asked, "What happened?" "Well the marriage didn't last, and I tried to get it covered up with a picture of Don Quixote." He explained that neither her name nor the picture of Don Quixote could be made out since the revision. No one could tell exactly what was on his ankle anymore, and he found himself reluctant to wear shorts because he was embarrassed by the big ink spot that seemed to attract attention anytime it was visible. I thought to myself: *Here was this good-looking man sitting in front of me who was permanently scarred because of a decision he made when he was nineteen.*

I understand that tattoos are considered sexy by some but, I assure you, you will be much happier in the long run if the tattoo you choose does not have a woman's name or likeness on it. Perhaps more to the point, more women will find you attractive if they see you haven't been "branded" by someone else. If a woman asks you to get a tattoo to prove your love for her, find another way to prove it. Too many people are running around with bad ink and even worse revisions--and much of that has to do with past relationships permanently inscribed on their bodies. Think before you ink and you'll be so much happier in the long run.

Cue Card: Try not to objectify every woman you meet.

If you can't help yourself from doing this, you will need to exercise some self-control and try harder to stop it. Even if you don't think anyone notices, trust me—they do. The woman you're objectifying will notice it, and everyone else will notice you doing this as well. No woman finds this behavior attractive. As much as you may like to believe women find this sexy, trust me--we don't. To be honest, we find it creepy. If you want women to find you more attractive, it helps if they don't think of you as a creepy predator.

To illustrate, there are some men who seem to leer at just about every woman they see. It doesn't seem to matter what type of women they are with or where they are—when a woman they find attractive walks by, they stare lecherously.

Let's be clear: This is not attractive to anyone and, quite honestly, this type of behavior can frighten people.

Cue Card: Go to the right places.

You can't expect to meet the type of woman you have in mind for yourself if you're not going to the places your perfect partner would likely visit, or by not doing the things that are likely to interest her. Let me illustrate. I worked with one patient who came to see me because he wanted to figure out why he kept on ending up in similar relationships that ultimately turned out to be unsuccessful. He longed for a wife and children, but now he was in his 40s and still had not met anyone. My first question to him was, "Where are you looking?" He told me he had been going to meet women at the same "hangout" he had frequented since his mid-twenties. I asked him if he had ever met women anywhere else. He said no. He explained that his relationships with the women he met at the club he frequented never seemed to endure. I jumped in and said, "Aren't these the relationships you've told me about that have always ended in disaster?" He said, "Yes." We stared at each other for a moment. He broke the silence. "Well, that doesn't seem to be working too well now does it?" I nodded in agreement and smiled.

Over the course of the next few sessions we talked about the types of qualities he wanted in a woman, and then we came up with a list of places he could go to start interacting with like-minded people who had similar interests. I am happy to report that he has been happily married now for the last five years. Gone are the dramatic arguments and bitter breakups, and the relationship he shares with his wife is so good that neither one of them needs counseling anymore. This patient became a true success story simply by getting smart with his search for a partner—you can easily do the same thing.

Cue Card: Don't be afraid to approach someone you're interested in.

It's always interesting to me that men, for the most part, seem pretty confident when you ask them how they feel about themselves. However, when it comes to introducing themselves to someone they're attracted to, this confidence seems to fall by the wayside. This may sound strange, but did you know that some of the most attractive and accomplished women are also among some of the loneliest women out there? The reason for this is that men are too intimidated to approach them and ask them for a date. Having talked to a number of women in this type of circumstance, they tell me they'd love it if a guy approached them and asked them out. The next time you see someone who interests you, go up to her, engage in some pleasant small talk, and ask her for her phone number. Don't let fear stand in your way--that's silly. The worst thing that will happen is that the woman will say she's involved with someone else or isn't currently on the dating market. Will you recover if someone tells you *no*? Of course, you will. Most likely, though, she'll be so happy you approached her that you'll probably be on a date with her within the next few days.

Cue Card: Take a class.

One of the largest ratios of single women to single men you will find is in an evening class at a community college or some other type of community recreation center. Even though it's easier to take courses online, you will most likely never meet anyone that way. A lot of single women take classes in things they're interested in during the evening and on weekends. When women are involved in a relationship, their free time is often spent with their significant other. When women are single, they often pursue other interests and work on self-improvement. An evening art, cooking, shop or even a foreign language class will most likely have lots of single women to mingle with. Also, taking a class together gives you and the person you're interested in a shared topic to discuss which often comes in handy during a first date. Taking a class also gives you a chance to get to know each other over a series of weeks and, in the meantime, you will be picking up a new skill. Give it a shot. You have absolutely nothing to lose and everything to gain.

Cue Card: Get (or borrow) a dog.

Many women love dogs and find a man who is walking his dog very appealing. Start walking your dog on a regular basis, and you'll be surprised how many women you meet and how many will actually come up and talk to you as they pet your furry friend. When you do it on a regular basis, you'll learn who is single and open to a new relationship. Soon, your conversations will become longer and you'll easily be able to work the conversation into a date request by asking, "Maybe we can take our dogs to the dog park sometime." When you're at the dog park together, ask for her phone number and then follow up by scheduling another date without your four-legged friends as chaperones.

Cue Card: Expand your in-person social network.

One of the best ways to meet women is to be introduced to them through your friends and family. When you meet a woman through a friend, it's like a pre-screening method so to speak--your friend knows you, your friend knows the woman they're going to introduce you to, and obviously your friend thinks you'd be compatible or you'd never be introduced to each other in the first place. The other added benefit of meeting someone through a friend is that you're likely to have more in common, so it gives you more opportunities to connect on a deeper level.

Cue Card: Expand your dating possibilities with dating websites.

If you live in a rural area, don't have time to enroll in classes, or don't want a dog, consider signing up for an online dating site. Three out of five couples today meet online. The good thing about meeting someone online is that it gives you a chance to see if your personalities are compatible *before* you meet. When choosing this option, I always recommend that you try to see the person that interests you in-person within three months. The reason for this is that as much as all of us would like to feel that everyone tells the truth, unfortunately there are a growing number of people who don't. Don't become a catfish victim. If a woman you're interested in avoids meeting you in person, you may want to consider looking for someone else to start a relationship with. I'm sure you've heard the stories of the things people try to hide--a man once shared a story with me that a woman he fell head over heels in love with ended up being another man pretending to be a woman. Don't be taken for a ride. If you're attracted to someone online, get to know each other a little, but put a time limit on exactly how long your relationship will remain online, and then make plans to meet in person.

Establishing a Connection

Now that you know how to meet women, use the set of Cue Cards below to help you establish a connection to the woman you would like to date.

Cue Card: Learn to be a good conversationalist by being a good listener.

You will be more effective in your communication with others if you learn how to truly listen, stay engaged in conversations, and let the other person know through your words and your actions that what they have to say is important to you. There is much more to being a good listener than nodding your head when someone speaks and offering the occasional grunt or groan that's supposed to indicate you're engaged. Really listening is an art comprised of many elements and, when done well, it helps you connect better with others.

Cue Card: Body language can be just as important as what is said.

Our communication with others is filled with lots of nonverbal information. Our tone, rhythm, and the volume at which we speak in conjunction with our body language, can reveal as much if not more than what we say. Your body language can indicate if you are sincere, curious, judgmental, or even bored. When you pay attention to another person's nonverbal communication, it will help you understand that person better. For example, in any of your previous relationships, has anyone ever looked angry or sad only to answer "I'm fine" when asked if anything is wrong? Of course, you probably would not want to approach someone you don't know very well about a significant disconnect between their words and their nonverbal communication, but as you get to know someone, it's okay to check out a discrepancy like the one described above. It may even help the person feel more at ease with you and, in turn, feel more open to sharing their true feelings.

Cue Card: Ask her about herself.

Another effective way to establish a connection with a woman (or anyone for that matter) is to start to get to know them, and the way to do this is by asking simple, open-ended questions. Of course, when you first meet a woman you are attracted to, you won't want to ask questions that may be considered personal, but rather more light-hearted questions like, "Are you from the area?" Or, "Do you come here often?" These are great ways to start engaging in casual chit-chat. As time passes, you can ask questions that are more personal in nature such as, "Are you married?" "What type of work do you do?" Most people like to talk about themselves, and by asking polite getting-to-know-you type of questions, you will start to learn things about one another that, in turn, will give more opportunities for conversation.

11

Cue Card: Hold off on mentioning the women from your past.

I assure you, no woman you are trying to develop a connection with wants to hear, "You remind me so much of my ex-wife or ex-girlfriend." Nor do they want the details about your exes. I'll never forget a first date I had with a man who in one sentence told me, "I hate my ex-wife," and in the next said, "You look so much like her." Needless to say, we didn't have a second date. Women like to feel special, and this feeling doesn't happen when we hear you talk about everyone from your past. Keep your attention in the present; if we want to know more about your relationship history, we'll ask you about it.

Chapter Two

Cue Cards for Dating

Now that you know how to meet women, let's talk about dating them. A first date won't lead to a second if you're not good at dating. If you've read the first chapter of this book, you're well on your way to being good at this, because so much of appealing to and attracting women has to do with the way you present yourself. However, even though you may present as a great package, to *keep* a woman's interest, you will need to be a good date. You'd be surprised at how many men just aren't. They're either boring, too aggressive, or too clingy. Remember: too much of anything is never good. In short, some men are just good at the chase, but that's about it. The Cue Cards in this chapter will help you be more successful in your dating.

The Basic Guidelines

Let the Cue Cards that follow serve as your ground rules for dating, and your relationship will be off to a great start.

Cue Card: Don't date someone to avoid being alone.

If you're feeling lonely, strive to build your network of friends rather than dating someone to fill the void in your life. If you date just to avoid being alone, the woman you get involved with will most likely be very hurt once you leave her after you find someone you're truly interested in. Nothing good usually comes from dating for convenience's sake. Save yourself (and your date) from heartache by finding more constructive ways to fill out your social calendar. Join a gym, learn a sport, or perhaps take a class in something that has always interested you to help you meet people with common interests.

Cue Card: Don't schedule more than one date a day.

Simply put, scheduling more than one date a day is a recipe for disaster. I don't care how good you are at making excuses to leave a current date, or how good you are with your time management skills, there will eventually be a time when you won't be able to keep your story straight and/or you'll run late. When this happens, not one woman involved with your time management crisis will want anything to do with you. Women want to feel special—that doesn't happen if we're only a stop in your schedule for the day.

Cue Card: If you're dating more than one woman at a time, be honest about it to all of them.

There's nothing wrong with dating more than one woman at a time, but there *is* something wrong in not being honest about it. Most women can sense when men are playing games with them. If you are dating more than one woman at a time--let *all* of them know. This way none of them can ever tell you later that they were misled. Some women will be okay with it and others won't, but you'll save yourself a lot of female hostility on the back end if you're upfront about how many women you are currently dating. As mentioned previously, women *do not* like to be played.

Cue Card: Put your best foot forward--show up on time and use your best social skills.

Nothing says you care less about a person than showing up late for a date. You'll be infinitely more attractive to your potential partner if you arrive when you're supposed to. When you're on time, you send the message that you're excited to see her and that you value your time together.

While out on your date, put your best social skills front and center. Be fun, engaging, and don't be distracted. Focus all of your attention on your date and try your best to have a good time.

Cue Card: Be aware of her boundaries and respect them.

We all learn, sooner or later, that people are different. You have things you are comfortable discussing and doing with others, and there are some things and topics that make you uncomfortable. The things that seem acceptable to you may not be the same for the person you're dating. Most of us have some subjects we simply do not discuss and things we simply won't do—even with our most trusted friends and family members. Just as you have personal beliefs, remember that others do too. Where we draw the line about the things we are willing to do and discuss and share with others is a boundary and, for successful and meaningful relationships, boundaries need to be respected, whether you agree with them or not.

There is no "one size fits all" approach to determining appropriate boundaries. They differ from person to person and are often influenced by social and cultural norms. If the woman you're dating is uncomfortable with something, don't try to make light of it or talk her into doing it. Try to pick up on the social or behavioral cues she is giving you as it will show her you are sensitive to her needs. When you respect another's boundaries, you send the message that you respect the person. When you try to push through someone's boundaries—even if it is with good intentions and in a joking way—at the very least, you will make the other person uncomfortable.

Cue Card: Power down and tune in.

You would be surprised how many people don't realize it's important to put your cell phone down when you're interacting with others face to face. If you want an immediate improvement in your relationship, put your electronic device away when you're spending time with someone. Don't get me wrong—I love cell phones and all that they offer, but what they very rarely do is make you closer as a couple. I see couples daily who are doing things together, but not engaged in conversation with one another because they are either texting someone or staring at their phone for some other reason. Studies repeatedly show there is a direct correlation between screen time and depression. Who needs that? Additionally, how will you get to know your date better if you're distracted by your personal communication device? When you're out on a date, put your device away and use the opportunity to form a deeper connection.

Cue Card: Mind your moods so she doesn't feel like she has to walk on eggshells around you.

Everyone has moods. Good, bad, or indifferent, moods are a fact of life. What differentiates adults from children is the ability to exercise impulse control and to articulate how we feel. Two-year-olds have tantrums because they do not possess the verbal skills to express their frustrations and pain. Teens are also notoriously moody. As we mature, though, we hopefully develop the vocabulary needed to express how we are feeling, and our brain develops the capacity to place a filter between what we think and what we say. Generally speaking, anyone over the age of twenty-one who is in good physical and mental health should be able to express how they feel in a socially appropriate manner and to refrain from emotional outbursts under most circumstances.

We are all probably guilty of a flaring temper at times of high stress, but when inconsistencies in mood become the norm rather than the exception, it's time to figure out what is causing your mood swings. If you want to draw a woman closer to you, you will have a better chance of doing so if you keep your mood swings to a minimum. Women don't like to feel they need to walk on eggshells around a man to avoid making him angry. Act and communicate like an adult if you want your relationship to grow. No one should ever be your emotional punching bag. Some temperamental people claim, "That's just the way I am." Well, this may be true, but if you want people to view you as an adult, you will need to get that behavior under control. If most one-year-olds can do it, so can you. Even-temperedness is attractive. Volatility is not.

Cue Card: If you don't currently plan on having children, use protection.

Most men will say they don't like the way condoms feel; however, they are highly effective in preventing pregnancy and sexually transmitted diseases. Even if a woman tells you she's taking the pill or using some other form of birth control, it's important to consider that she may have missed a dose earlier in the month, she may be taking some other medication that may make her birth control pills less effective, and/or she is not using another form of birth control correctly. Did you know antibiotics render birth control pills less effective? It's true. If you don't want to have children with the woman you are with, be responsible for yourself and use protection. Even though you may not like the feel of a condom, I assure you that you will like the feeling of eighteen years of child support even less.

Show Her You're a Good Guy

If you want one date to lead to the next, it will be in your best interests to show her you're someone she'd like to keep in her life. The Cue Cards below will help you do this.

Cue Card: Make her feel beautiful.

Women love men who make them feel beautiful. Have you ever wondered why a guy who has less to offer than you do has a really attractive woman at his side? It's most likely because he knows how to work what he has—and sometimes that can just be his words. A lot of men make the very common mistake of only turning on the charm with their woman if they want sex. What most men don't seem to understand is that women operate on a much longer sexual time clock. For the majority of women, foreplay happens 24 hours a day. We want to feel desired by you all the time. The best way to show this is verbalizing your feelings. No one is a mind reader. If you think a woman looks nice--tell her. Flirt with her regularly. She'll be much more amenable to your advances if she feels you find her attractive *all* the time.

Cue Card: Don't embarrass her in front of her friends or her family.

One of the worst things any man can do is make a woman look bad in front of her friends and family. Remember, when you are with someone and her friends or family are around, her friends and family are judging you on what they see *at the time they see you.* Even though you may treat her great 99% of the time and may have just had one bad day that happens to occur when you're around the people closest to her, it's *that* day that the others will hold on to, because that's the most recent, in-person impression they have of you. Help the woman in your life look better to the people who are important to her by treating her with kindness and respect when she is with others she cares about--she'll love you even more for it. And who knows? If her mom ends up liking you, she could be a very good ally to you for many years to come.

Have you ever witnessed one member of a couple loudly criticizing the other in public? I think people sometimes forget that what they find offensive in their partner may go unnoticed by others. Criticizing your partner in front of her family not only makes her feel bad, it draws attention to the perceived problem. Again, it's important to remember that her friends and family only see you interact as a couple for a limited time. If they observe you criticizing, or in some other way treating her with disrespect, they may think your relationship is like that all the time. If you demonstrate that you like and respect your partner, her family and friends will perceive your relationship in a good light which can only have a positive impact for the two of you going forward.

Cue Card: Don't try to make your girlfriend jealous.

There is nothing wrong with finding other women attractive, but there *is* something wrong if you decide to flirt with one of them. In my practice and in real life, I have often seen couples who seem to make it a sport to make each other jealous. Then they complain that their partner is either possessive or insecure. It's almost as though the instigating partner fails to see their own role in creating this problem. In my opinion, if you're the one trying to stir up jealousy in your relationship, it's *you* who has the problem. People who are happy and secure do not need constant affirmations that others find them attractive. If you are secure and content with yourself, there is no reason to continually seek the affirmation of others (and yes, that includes exchanging suggestive comments and pictures on social media—even if you've never met the person you're doing this with, it still counts). If you are insecure with something about yourself, take strides to fix it. Don't try to make your partner jealous.

One of the least attractive qualities you can display when you're dating someone is checking out other women when you are out together. Let me make it clear again that it's perfectly normal to look at other attractive women—however, it is disrespectful to do it when you are on a date with the woman you care about. If you truly care about your partner, making them jealous will not bring you two closer.

Cue Card: Leave your road rage at the curb.

When you're driving with a woman you care about, or anyone else for that matter, you will totally destroy the mood in the car (and probably for the rest of the date), if you have a fit of road rage. No one likes to feel that a fist fight is going to occur on the side of the road. There will always be horrible drivers and people who drive aggressively for what seems like no reason at all. That said, there's no reason *you* need to react to it. I know this is easier said than done, but why waste your time together making yourself look bad over a terrible driver? Show your better side and keep your road rage in check.

Cue Card: Treat the waiter (or anyone else who's helping you) with respect and dignity.

Little interactions you have with others give glimpses of your true personality. You may not think that your interaction with a waiter can reveal a lot about you, and you may not think that anyone is watching you interact with the wait staff at a restaurant, but you need to know you are wrong on both accounts. If you treat the waiter poorly, you are in essence telling the others around you (not to mention the waiter), that you have a disrespectful streak in you and, perhaps, a sense of entitlement. Even though you may feel you are a very important person, it doesn't mean that others are *less important than you*. Everyone deserves to be treated with respect. Women watch for little things like this (as do employers). When you the treat people you have nothing to gain from disrespectfully, others who observe this quickly learn that you're only nice to people when you want something from them.

Cue Card: Don't play power games.

Testing a relationship, regardless of what stage it is in, is silly and immature. If you can't help yourself from doing it, try to figure out what's missing inside yourself so you don't need to do it anymore. Power games include: trying to make women jealous, the silent treatment (for any reason), doing things to purposely make her angry, spying on her, stalking her, keeping her from her friends and family, putting her down, insulting her in public (or insulting her any other time for that matter), nitpicking her behaviors, withholding emotional support, and purposely not taking an interest in her life.

Doesn't that list just sound unappealing? The reason it does is because it *is*. Hang up the need to play games because, at the end of the day, it gets you nowhere and makes you a person impossible to have a healthy relationship with. A man who is secure in himself will not feel a need to exercise control over a woman.

Relationship Builders

Continue to grow closer to the person you're dating by using the Cue Cards below to help build your relationship.

Cue Card: Pay attention to the cues she gives you.

Women find it very attractive when a man not only listens to them but goes the extra mile to act on the information he's given. Hear what she's saying and don't just nod your head in agreement and make token grunts and groans pretending you're in tune with her. If she tells you she likes something--remember it. If she tells you she likes to go to a certain place--go there. It takes minimal effort to show you're paying attention to the things she's seeking in a relationship. Women express their desires for a reason. Trust me, if you don't fulfill them, the first person who walks into her life and does so will be the person she ultimately ends up with.

Cue Card: Show her you care by taking an interest in things that are important to her.

You don't necessarily have to love going shopping and getting manicures on Saturdays, but if she has a cause, hobby, or even a family member or friend who is important to her, try to take at least *some* interest in a few of the things that are important to her. As women, we are actually on the whole very good at taking an interest in the things that are important to the men that we are romantically interested in. We do it to show you we care for you and as a way to bond with you. Conversely, when you take an interest in what's important to *us*, we feel we're important to *you* (and that's just something we find very sexy).

Cue Card: Draw her closer to you by showing her you are someone she can rely on.

Once you are in a relationship, it will help if you view your relationship as a *partnership*. You know how it's been told that when men go to war they watch out for their buddy's back? If you adopt this mindset for your relationship, you will be so much better off. When she has a bad day, be there for her to offer support and a non-judgmental ear to vent to. If she needs help with something, offer to supply the help that she needs. When the woman in your life feels you have her back no matter what, she will most likely reciprocate. Adopting a partnership mindset will help provide a strong foundation for your growing relationship.

Cue Card: When you get her a gift, get her a gift she would like--not what you think she should have.

You may think the woman in your life could really use an air compressor in the event her tires are low and you're not around to help, but I encourage you to think twice about this gift. Though there are some women who would actually like it, most probably would not consider an air compressor a romantic gift. For the most part, it isn't all that difficult to figure out what women like...all it takes is a little effort to pay attention to details. Does she talk about any type of gift? Are shoes her thing? Does she like video games? Has she been eyeing a new fitness tracker? Is there a concert she's been wanting to see? When was the last time she had a spa day? Most women will reveal the things they like--you just need to pay some attention and notice them. If you can't seem to figure out what she likes, consider getting her a gift certificate for a massage or planning a weekend trip to a place she has always wanted to go. A lot of men make the mistake of thinking that gifts have to be expensive to mean something to women--it's not true. Most women will find a thoughtful gift more meaningful than an expensive gift; so, in most cases, dollar amounts are irrelevant. One of the best gifts my husband ever gave me was a hand-made jewelry box. I could tell he had spent many hours constructing it. He even went so far as to have a small plaque for it custom engraved for me. When I opened it, he explained that he listened to the way I always admired unique handcrafted gifts, and how I loved exotic woods. To date, that jewelry box is one of my most treasured possessions. Show the woman in your life you're thoughtful and make her happier by giving her the gift *she* would like-- not the gift *you* think she should have.

Cue Card: Manage your exes.

If you're the type of guy who gets a kick out of women fighting over him, you may want to find another way to enjoy yourself if you truly want to meet someone and have a lasting relationship with her. Out of respect for the woman you are involved with, you should be sensitive to how *she* feels about you being in contact with your exes. Of course, if you have a child with a former partner, that's a different story and will be addressed in another Cue Card. But if there are no children involved, you may want to show some consideration as to how the current lady of your life feels about you being in contact with women from your past. Many women aren't comfortable with the "we're just friends now" mindset. The reason for this is that, for women, it's very important for most of us to feel that what we have with our partner is special. If what we have with you is something *she* had with you--plus *she* has history on her side, we're not really going to feel that we are all that special to you anymore. If it's important to you to remain friends with a former girlfriend, and the woman you are currently involved with is uncomfortable with the idea, see if perhaps you can seek some type of compromise that works for both of you. If you are not able to reach a mutually agreeable solution, then it may be time to reconsider your current relationship for both of your sakes.

Cue Card: Be honest about significant issues you've had in your past.

If you're lying about something from your past for fear of her reaction, it's time to confess, because whatever it is you're hiding, she *will* eventually find out. A common thing a lot of men don't seem to realize is that when we catch you lying, we eventually become suspicious *of everything you say and do*. It may not be right, but that's the way most of us think.

I have never met a woman who didn't value honesty in a man. If you are being dishonest about something in your life, sit down and lay it all out--the good, the bad, and the ugly. If you have a history of the following things: substance abuse, alcohol abuse, domestic violence (even if it was just "once or twice"), poor credit, promiscuity, multiple marriages, children, sexually transmitted diseases, etc., you *must* be forthcoming with all of this information to your intended partner when things start to get serious.

As much as I recommend putting your past behind you, and as much as *you* would like to do so and forget certain events ever even happened, your past is part of what defines who you are today. If you have a history of substance abuse or alcohol abuse, your partner needs to know that, because most people who have this type of history are susceptible to having issues with these things again. The same thing goes for any other addiction or problem—we tend to be creatures of habit, and as the saying goes: The best predictor of future behavior is past behavior. If you try to hide this type of information, I can just about promise you that one day you will regret your decision to do so. Although it may be difficult, please know it will ultimately be healthier for your relationship to have the difficult conversations about your past *now*—before your relationship gets any more serious. Your partner deserves to know the truth about you, just as you deserve to know the truth about her. Let me illustrate why this is important: Let's say you date someone who *loves* to go to Las Vegas, and you have a history of gambling addiction. At the very least, you owe your partner an explanation as to why a trip to Vegas may be difficult for you. Also, consider this: One of the qualities you will ideally look for in a serious partner is someone who is sensitive to your needs--the woman you are with will not be able to be sensitive to your needs if she doesn't know what they are. This is why it's important to be honest about *everything*. Again, this means things such as past marriages, children you may have, your credit history and domestic violence, it is imperative you are open and honest about all of your significant past history. The *other* reason for this is that your partner has a right to know who she is getting involved with just as much as you have a right to know who she is. If this is still difficult for you to understand, look at it conversely: If you fell madly in love with a woman and were getting serious and eventually married her, how would you feel if say ten years down the road you found out she was a prostitute in her youth? What if she had a series of sex tapes that somehow leaked on the internet? While some of these things may not bother some men, it would probably bother at least a few of you. I like to refer to this type of disclosure as Informed Consent. You owe it to your partner (just as much as your partner owes it to you) to be honest and reveal exactly the type of person she is getting involved with. If you have a colorful past, it doesn't necessarily mean your partner will no longer want to be involved with you, but it will be *her* decision to make once she has all the facts.

When you talk about these things, I encourage you to be delicate without being evasive. It's not necessary to divulge every detail of every sexual encounter you have but, let's put it this way, if you feel you would want to know certain details about your partner, you should be willing to share similar details. Exercise good judgment and respect your partner enough to let her make a fully informed decision about whether or not she wants to stay with you. Your partnership will ultimately grow to be much stronger when it is built on a foundation of truth.

Cue Card: Be careful about who you "friend" on social media.

I can't think of too many women (or men) who are okay with their partner having lots of friends who post provocative photos of themselves on social media. Even worse are the "flirty/sexy" messages you may be sharing with these people. Here are two good rules of thumb to follow with social media: 1) If you wouldn't like it if you knew your partner was doing the same type of thing with the opposite gender, then you probably shouldn't be doing it either; 2) If your partner finds out who your friends are and how you've been interacting with them, will she be okay with it? If the answer to either question is *no*, then it's probably a wise idea to revise your friend list and re-think your online interactions.

Cue Card: Don't be controlling.

If you feel you need to monitor your partner's comings and goings, on-line interactions, texts, and emails, you may want to ask yourself why you feel this way. I can assure you that no matter how closely you monitor someone, if a person is going to be unfaithful to you, they will be unfaithful to you regardless of what measures you take to make sure it doesn't happen. If you are monitoring everything in your partner's life, you may want to ask yourself if you really want to be with someone who makes you feel so insecure. Also, remember that in relationships, sometimes when you hold on too tightly to someone you will actually create the behavior you're trying to prevent and thus drive the person you care about most away from you. Be careful of emotionally suffocating someone you care about due to your own insecurities.

When Things Don't Work Out

We date people to find out if we're compatible or not. If, after some time, you find that things aren't working out in your dating relationship, it may be time to stop seeing each other. If you decide to breakup, let the Cue Cards below help you make your breakup as painless as possible.

Cue Card: If it's over, tell her and be kind about it.

If you're dating someone and you feel you don't want to see her again—let her know. Be honest, direct, and be kind—but be direct. It may hurt her more up front, but it will actually hurt her less than putting "polite distance" between the two of you, or completely ghosting her in the hope that she will get the hint that you no longer want to see her anymore. Look at it this way, the sooner you tell her, the sooner she'll be able to move on with her life, too.

Cue Card: If she tells you the relationship is over, believe that she means it.

Just as you have the ability to decide if you want to continue dating someone, she has the ability to decide if she would like to continue to date *you*. It's quite normal to be hurt after a breakup—especially if you are not the initiator of it; but in time your feelings (and ego) will heal. One of the worst things you can do if a woman tells you she is no longer interested in dating you is to not let her go. A guy who is clingy is unattractive to most women and, if this describes you, all you will be doing if you continue to chase her after she's told you it's over is prove to her that she made the right decision. On the whole, women don't come to the decision to end a relationship lightly—even a dating relationship. So, when she tells you it's over, she means it. Keep your dignity intact and accept her ending things as gracefully as possible.

Cue Card: Don't be physically abusive—ever.

If you have difficulty expressing your anger without being verbally abusive or physically violent, the truth is that you should not be in any type of dating or intimate relationship. It is *never* okay to hit, slap, kick, bite, or in any other manner hurt, threaten, or intimidate another person when you are angry or frustrated. It is also never acceptable to destroy another person's property, regardless of how angry you are at them. If you are unable to express your anger, frustration, hurt, or any other emotion without resorting to violence or destruction of property, please seek help from a licensed mental health professional. Don't be ashamed or embarrassed about seeking professional help to assist you in learning how to express emotions without violence and destruction. You will have much healthier relationships of all kinds when you learn to express yourself without harming others. No one should ever drive you to the point of physical violence and, if you feel they do, you shouldn't be around that person long enough to act on it. This goes for the woman in your life too—if she's physically violent with you, it's *not* okay.

If you are the victim of domestic violence, immediately call the police. Also, please consider seeking the assistance of a licensed mental health professional to help you learn how to select emotionally healthier romantic partners. If you're in an abusive relationship, please see the Resources section at the end of this book for websites and phone numbers to assist you in getting the help you or your partner needs. It doesn't matter if it's a man or woman who instigates violence—no one who cares about you should ever physically hurt you. It is *never* okay for either gender to be abusive.

If you think you can't afford counseling, I can share with you that there are lower cost counseling options available. If you live in an area where there are colleges and universities offering graduate degrees in psychology, they will most likely have some type of mental health clinic on campus where students are working toward earning their internship hours needed for graduation and eventual licensure. At these clinics, mental health services are performed by interns and supervised by Licensed Clinicians, and they usually offer reduced rate counseling services to the public or base their fees on your ability to pay. Because there is a great need for low cost counseling, availability is often limited, and there could be a waiting list, so you may have to wait a little while before you get an appointment. But on the positive side, once you make the appointment, you will be taking a step in the right direction toward helping yourself. If you don't live in an area that has colleges and universities, consider contacting your county's department of health services and asking them to refer you to a place that offers counseling at a reduced fee. At the end of this book I have also included a list of counseling websites to assist you in getting the help you need. Help is out there for you—don't be afraid to get it.

Cue Card: Don't stalk her.

If you think the woman you're stalking will find your obsessiveness attractive, think again—she won't. Your actions will most likely drive her even further away. No one likes to have someone looking over their shoulder or be startled when finding out that someone is tracking her every move.

To be clear, according to the Stalking Resource Center at the National Center for Victims of Crime, stalking is defined as a pattern of repeated and unwanted attention, harassment, contact, or any other course of conduct directed at a specific person that would cause a reasonable person to feel fear. Stalking behaviors can include:

Repeated, unwanted, intrusive, and frightening communications from the perpetrator by phone, mail, and/or email;

Repeatedly leaving or sending the victim unwanted items, presents, or flowers;

Following or lying in wait for the victim at places such as home, school, work, or places of recreation;

Making direct or indirect threats to harm the victim, the victim's children, relatives, friends, or pets;

Damaging or threatening to damage the victim's property;

Harassing a victim through the internet;

Posting information or spreading rumors about the victim on the internet, in a public place, or by word of mouth;

Obtaining personal information about the victim by accessing public records, using internet search services, hiring private investigators, going through the victim's garbage, following the victim, contacting victim's friends, family, work, or neighbors, etc.

If you're doing any of these things—or thinking about doing any of these things—stop it now or you just may end up in jail. If you find that you can't stop doing these things, then it's time to seek some help for your behavior from a Licensed Mental Health Professional. For your convenience, I have included a list of therapist directories at the end of this book to assist you in getting you the help you need. Again, help is available to you, so if you need it please don't be embarrassed about seeking it. It's not weak to ask for help, and the sooner you get it, the sooner you'll be on the road to happiness again.

Chapter Three

Cue Cards for Your Engagement and Wedding

Y ou've dated someone for a while now and, instead of getting bored with your time together, you find that you want to see her more and more as your feelings for her grow. Every so often you even start having fleeting thoughts of marriage. Is it time to ask her to marry you? It very well could be. In this chapter you'll find Cue Cards that will help you decide if the time is right and, if it is, this chapter will even walk you through the big day. If it's not your first trip down the aisle, this set of Cue Cards will help make sure it's your *last* trip—because this time you'll get it right.

Know When You're Ready

Cue Card: Don't rush into making the decision to take your relationship to the next level.

One of the best things you can do before you decide to get engaged is to date the person you're with for at least a year. The reason for this is that most people—men and women alike—are on their best behavior for the first year of a relationship. After the twelve-month mark, people get more relaxed with one another, and you'll be able to glimpse aspects of their personality that you may not have seen before. At twelve months and beyond, you can truly get a good idea if the person you are considering marrying is someone you will be compatible with on a long-term basis. As tempting as it may be to rush into marriage earlier than twelve months, realize that much of the headiness you feel during the initial stages of a relationship is due to a chemical reaction in your brain to new love. Here's the science behind it: When you're in love, you experience activity in the right caudate nucleus and right ventral tegmental area dopamine, both of which have high levels of dopamine activity. Dopamine is a brain chemical which produces feelings of satisfaction and pleasure and, when dopamine levels are elevated, you feel increased energy and a generalized feeling of elation. More simply stated, your thinking is a little clouded during the first year of your romance because you basically have a dopamine rush going on. Give you and your intended spouse a chance to see each other in a more realistic light by letting these twelve months of headiness pass, and you'll have a much better chance of seeing your relationship potential for what it truly is.

Cue Card: Make a list and check it twice.

As unromantic as this may sound, making a list of the qualities that you feel are important in a life partner can help you make sure you're seeing your relationship objectively and not acting purely on emotion. A lot of men don't believe they get swept up in the moment, but trust me— they do and, when this happens, they usually make decisions they later regret. Is a wife who has an education important to you? What about a spouse who has a demanding career— are you okay with that? Do you want a partner who cooks? What if she doesn't want to work? Expecting to change a person on fundamental issues that you differ on *never* works and will only breed anger and resentment which could eventually cost you your marriage. There are no right or wrong qualities to desire in a mate—the important thing is that you are honest with yourself and know what you can live with and what you can't.

Cue Card: Be honest about your feelings and desires for children.

Some men love kids and others don't; but whatever side of the fence you fall on, you will need to have this conversation with your significant other *before* you take your relationship to the next level. Individuals seldom change from their desires for children, so if you're expecting to marry someone and convince her to have or *not* have kids, you are doing both of you a great disservice. This is an issue that is never resolved with a hope that one or the other person will "change his/her mind." If you are adamant that you do want children or that you don't, you will save you and your partner a lot of heartache if you find someone who shares your feelings on this very important topic.

Cue Card: Take both of your families into consideration.

How does your family feel about the person you are considering marrying? How does her family feel about you? You may not care what your family thinks about your future spouse, but how does your *fiancé* feel about it? What if they don't like her and are consistently unkind to her? Are you willing to confront your family and tell them that, even if they don't like your spouse-to-be, it is expected that they maintain a level of civility around her and treat her respectfully? Conversely, how would you feel if this situation was reversed?

Families of origin have the ability to cause an enormous amount of stress and strain even in the strongest of marriages. There is no right or wrong answer to how you should feel about your family's opinion about your spouse-to-be, but I guarantee you, there *will* be a problem if they don't treat your wife right and you don't stand up to them and ask them to treat her better. Part of marrying someone is becoming a new family unit (regardless if you have children or not). In such, if your family doesn't like your spouse or uses what I refer to as subtle "exclusionary tactics" (e.g., asking to her to step out of frame because they want a picture with "just the family"), there's a high probability your wife won't be okay with this kind of behavior regardless of how subtle your family thinks they are being in their actions. When that happens, you'll need to be prepared to stand up to your family and ask them to treat your wife better. If you're not prepared to do this, you are not ready to get married.

Cue Card: To prenup or not to prenup? That is the question.

If you're a little older and have accumulated some assets such as a house or a substantial savings account, a prenuptial agreement is something you may want to consider having. Is it unromantic? In my opinion, yes. On the other hand, is it a wise thing to do? Again, in my opinion—yes. It would be great to assume that all marriages will last forever but, in today's world, statistically, that's just not the case. With divorce rates hovering around fifty percent, having a prenuptial agreement may not be a bad idea if you have assets you would like to protect in the event you divorce. If you do decide on a prenuptial agreement, one thing you will need to consider is what you will do if your spouse-to-be refuses to sign it. Will you forgo the agreement? Will you end your engagement? Conversations around prenuptial agreements can be very emotional. Some women will understand where you are coming from while others won't. There is no right or wrong answer in regard to having a prenuptial agreement, and there is no right or wrong response to the request to sign one. It will all come down to the two individuals involved, and you will need to decide if this will be a "make or break" point for the future of your relationship.

Cue Card: Make your ring her thing.

You may want to surprise her with an engagement ring, but have you given much thought to the fact that while she may say yes to your proposal, that she may *not* like the ring you choose for her? Believe me, it happens more often than you know. As women, we know what looks good on us when it comes to clothes *and* jewelry. If you don't want to reveal your plans to her, spend an afternoon shopping online with her, or take her shopping on a street that has a lot of jewelry stores and playfully window shop. Tell her you're looking for a present for your mom or sister to throw her further off the trail from figuring out what you're up to. Then, when you're "window shopping," pay attention to the jewelry styles that catch her eye and listen closely to any verbal indications she makes. (I have met very few women who do not have an opinion on things when they look at jewelry.) For an additional safeguard, check to see if the store has a return or exchange policy that would allow you to bring her ring back in the event she would like something different.

Cue Card: Ask her to marry you in a way she'll never forget.

Now that you've considered all of the necessary (albeit unromantic) components of asking someone to marry you, here is the fun part—the proposal. Ideally, you'll do this in a way that will increase your odds of getting a "yes" answer, combined with a way in which she'll remember the moment for the rest of her life. Be creative, be romantic, and have fun with your proposal. If you're typically not a romantic type of guy and tend to look at anything romantic as fluff, give yourself a break when it comes to your proposal and pull out all the romantic stops—most women will love you even more for doing so. An unforgettable proposal doesn't need to be expensive; it just needs to be creative and heartfelt. Here are some ideas to help you start thinking in the right direction...

When you are running errands together, take a detour to park and have a picnic basket ready to go in the trunk of your car. Propose to her during your picnic.

Come home a little early from work and prepare a romantic dinner table for two in front of your fireplace.

Light candles, prepare her favorite meal, and propose over dinner.

If adventure is more her thing, plan to propose at a scenic setting during a hike.

If you two are flying anywhere in the near future, ask the flight attendant to ask the pilot if he'd make an announcement on the airplane's sound system—she'll be totally surprised!

Wedding Planning

Planning your big day may be very stressful, but if you use the Cue Cards that follow, you may be less stressed. And who knows? You may even find the process enjoyable.

Cue Card: Take an active interest in your wedding planning.

As easy and fun as wedding planning looks on television and online, let me be completely honest with you and share with you that it will probably be one of the more stressful—and in some cases—perhaps one of the most unpleasant experiences of your lives. Many issues arise during wedding planning: finances, scheduling, family conflict. It can make for the perfect storm of unpleasantness. In fact, in some cases, wedding planning becomes so unpleasant that it has ended relationships before couples ever make it down the aisle. As much as you may roll your eyes at the thought of picking flowers and wedding invitations, your fiancée may need your support. On the brighter side, ideally you will only get married one time in your life so the good news is that you will only have to go through the wedding planning process once.

Your participation in every aspect of wedding planning may not be all that important to your fiancée, but it would be good to let her know that you are there for her if she needs you. For me, personally, it wasn't important to have my husband involved, and I know that there are other women who feel the same way. My best tip is for you to figure out your role in planning your wedding (unless of course you have strong opinions about participating in the planning yourself) and be direct about it. Ask your fiancée exactly how involved she would like you to be and what expectations she has of you during this time. This way both of you can be clear with your expectations of each other and save a lot of tension and, hopefully, avoid unnecessary arguments down the road. Of course, her needs could change over time and, if they do, be flexible and strive to be as supportive as you can. Planning a wedding is good practice in teamwork—a skill you will definitely need once you are married.

Cue Card: Keep your family in check during the wedding planning process.

Emotions run high during wedding planning, and many of you will find that all kinds of relatives—even some you haven't heard from in years—will have opinions and demands of you and your fiancée. The demands family members put on couples during this time can be enormously stressful and the source of many (sometimes heated) arguments. Family situations can quickly spin out of control. So, if your family is the "offending party" in causing problems in your wedding, it is *your* responsibility to keep their behavior in check. While they may not like it when you put limits on their behavior, your loyalty should lie with your future spouse—not the family member who is causing the grief.

Cue Card: Come up with a mutual agreement about Bachelor and Bachelorette Parties.

In my years of counseling couples, I've seen many problems, and even some wedding cancellations, arise from arguments couples have around bachelor and bachelorette parties.

If your partner is not okay with you going to a strip club—don't do it. Is a night of bumping and grinding really worth the months of anguish you will be putting your spouse through (or all the months *you* will have to apologize for your actions)? If you find that going to a strip club is something you must do for your bachelor party and it's something that your fiancé is adamantly against, you may want to re-evaluate your relationship and see if you are marrying the right person.

Bachelor and bachelorette parties are often great and fun things to do, but I strongly encourage you to come up with a mutual plan about what you both have in mind to do at your individual parties. A lot of men get so wrapped up with their buddies planning their party, they seem to forget that their fiancée may have an equally wild party planned. For you guys who don't think bachelorette parties get as wild as some bachelor parties, think again—very good-looking male strippers in skimpy thongs, bump, grind, and kiss the women who are open to it—and sometimes even *more* happens.

Each member of a couple has boundaries regarding what they are comfortable with their partner doing. Some couples are fine with strippers, and some are not. There's no such thing as "normal" when it comes to boundaries. Simply stated, if it is your boundary, or your partner's boundary, it should be considered normal. Save yourself a lot of heartache, and quite possibly your relationship, by being honest with your partner about your bachelor party plans. Come to terms both of you can live with and stick to your agreement.

The Big Day

The next set of Cue Cards will help increase your chances of having a flawless wedding day.

Cue Card: Rest up the night before—you've got a long day ahead of you.

Wedding days usually start fairly early during the day and end late in the evening. Don't use the night before your wedding to have one last night out with the guys. Trust me, you'll need all your energy and a clear head the following day. A restful sleep will help you handle any stress or anxiety you may be feeling more effectively, and it will help you enjoy and remember your big day.

Cue Card: Don't drink too much before, during, or after your wedding.

Your wedding will probably be one of the most important things that happens in your life. As fun as weddings can be, they are—as mentioned previously—also extremely stressful. It can be overwhelming to think about making a lifetime commitment to another person and all the responsibility that goes with it. On top of all the emotions and stress you'll be feeling on the big day, most likely there will be alcohol readily available too. Bluntly, this could be a recipe for disaster—not only for you, but for your bride, your family, her family, and usually just about anyone else in attendance. Of course, it's okay for most people to imbibe at their wedding, but if you're using alcohol to "take the edge off," be careful—while you're taking the edge off, you could be getting more intoxicated than you think you are. The combination of alcohol and stress could lead you to do a lot of things you'll regret and, worse yet, there will probably be photos and videos of what transpires, so you'll never be able to fully forget about any social missteps. Watch the alcohol, don't get into silly arguments, and try to make your wedding day as pleasant as possible.

Cue Card: Make sure your Best Man really is the best man for the job.

The person you select to be your Best Man will have a direct reflection on the type of person you are. Therefore, it would be a wise thing to choose a Best Man who will not make you look bad on one of the most important days of your life. If you have any doubts or concerns about what your Best Man may say during his speech, ask him to run the speech by you before he makes it. If you don't like something he plans to say, feel free to tell him so, and if he doesn't want to remove it, know that it's okay to remove him from the toasting line up. The last thing you want on a day like this is to have your buddy talk about all of your old girlfriends, recant less than stellar moments from your past, or be someone who doesn't even remember your new wife's name (yes, it happens). A good majority of your relatives will be in attendance, as well as your wife's family—this is a day you should look good to everyone, and if your Best Man is truly your friend, he will understand and help you accomplish that.

Cue Card: Send your wife-to-be a little gift before she walks down the aisle.

One of the most sentimental and unforgettable things you can do for your future spouse is to take a little extra time to send something to her as she's getting ready. It doesn't need to be expensive or elaborate, just sweet and sentimental. It can be a single long stem rose, a little hand written note, or maybe even a small piece of jewelry. This little action lets her know you are thinking of her and sends the message in a romantic way that you two are a team. Not many men do this, and it's probably because they don't have the "insider information" from a woman which you are now lucky to possess because you're reading this book. I've never met a woman who didn't appreciate this type of thoughtful gesture.

Chapter Four

Cue Cards for Marriage and Fatherhood

Congratulations on your engagement and wedding and welcome to life as a married man. At this point, you probably think you're on the easier side of things when it comes to your relationship. After all, you've gone through all the dating phases, met her family, introduced her to yours, and walked down the aisle. What could be left? I'm sure you're thinking you can finally return to your day-to-day business with a sense of normalcy and, for the most part, you can. While it's true you and your new spouse will no longer have to worry about all the stress that goes into planning a wedding, the real work on your relationship is now just beginning. In general, people put an enormous amount of effort into walking down the aisle. Then, once they are married, they're often surprised to find that marriage requires a completely different set of relationship skills for it to survive. Some couples seem to entirely lack this set of what I like to call "relationship endurance skills." It's not that the skills are all that difficult, but if you didn't have a chance to learn them growing up—either because your parents had a bad relationship, or you just didn't pay any attention—I can almost promise you that you will struggle with the *staying* married part of your relationship.

In this chapter, you'll find Cue Cards that will help you develop and/or refresh your skills for staying married and, probably more importantly, these skills will help you stay *happily* married. Later in the chapter, I'll transition into Cue Cards for Fatherhood for those of you who plan to have children. Being a good father—just like marriage—is another completely different skill set. Don't worry though, easy help is here for you and, once you learn these Cue Cards, you'll be well on your path toward a very happy married life and, if children are in your future, you'll be well on your way to becoming a great dad.

Marriage

Newly married life, while mostly blissful, can still present a unique set of issues that you may be unprepared for. Use the Cue Cards below to help you brush up on (or re-learn) your *Husband 101* skills.

Cue Card: The relationship with your wife outranks all of your other relationships.

Now that you are married, you and your spouse are a team. The simple concept here is to approach life together, be there for each other when you stumble, help each other to do your best, and *never* give your life partner reason to question your loyalty. If you have difficulty conceptualizing this, think of my example of men in combat—these are the exact same things they do for each other. If you approach your marriage in this same manner, you'll increase the chances of your marriage standing the test of time exponentially.

Cue Card: Never stop dating your wife and help keep the spark alive.

It's very easy to start taking each other for granted once you get married. You can easily avoid this by continuing to date your wife. Go out for dinner once a week; go for a walk and hold hands; take a drive to the beach or mountains. Do the things you normally did when you dated. When you continue to date your wife, you strengthen your bond with her, and it also lets her know you still desire her in a romantic way—not just as a person who makes you an occasional sandwich and picks up your socks when you leave them on the floor. In turn, this will help her feel closer and more attracted to you. Always keep in mind that it's very hard to stay attracted to someone who takes you for granted. If you want to feel your wife still desires you, she needs to feel the same from you and you can continue to foster this feeling by dating-type behaviors. Also, shared experiences are one of the best things you can do to strengthen your relationship, because it gives you good memories to look back on when things get tough. Later, if you decide to have kids, dating your wife will be a great behavior for you to role model to your children. You'll be teaching them the dynamics of a healthy relationship. In short, dating is the gift that keeps on giving.

Cue Card: Don't hold back on expressing your emotions to your partner.

There are some men who seem to think that the display of any emotion other than anger isn't masculine. Let me share something with you: when you don't show love, compassion, understanding, happiness, sadness, or any other emotion I've left out, your partner will eventually think you don't care about her. I'm not saying you have to cry while watching a romantic movie or applaud with enthusiasm when she shows you a new outfit but showing a *little* emotion on a consistent basis is never a bad thing. As mentioned, it lets her know you are actually in tune to what is going on and that you care about her. I'm also not saying that you have to be excited about everything she's excited about, but you can let her know you are interested in *her* by expressing emotion from time to time. If she looks nice, tell her. If she's done a great job with the kids, tell her. If you love her, tell her—and tell her often. If you are angry, tell her that as well—just do it respectfully.

Cue Card: Safeguard Your Marriage from an Affair

Men and women don't always value the same things in a relationship. When this is the case, you may be—in your mind—trying your best to show your love to your partner only to find yourself feeling frustrated because she seems indifferent to your efforts. You think to yourself, "I am doing X all day long to make her happy, but she doesn't appreciate it." In time, you grow resentful and angry and feel she takes you for granted. Do you know why you're doing X all day and she doesn't care? It's because what she really wants is Y. Let me give you a real-life example. My husband and I are very good friends with Susan and Paul. We've known them for over ten years and shared a lot of laughs and memories together. My husband, Rusty, and I always felt that Susan and Paul had a great relationship like we do. Together they seemed happy and neither one of them had ever had a negative thing to say about the other. Imagine my surprise one afternoon over lunch with Susan when she told me she and Paul were having problems. "How can that be?" I asked. "He seems crazy about you." She sighed and looked sad when she said, "I just don't feel like we connect anymore." "Why is that?" I asked. She said that while Paul was a great dad to their kids and worked hard to provide a nice life for their family, she said she'd be happier with fewer material things if he'd just take her by the hand every so often and tell her she's pretty. "Have you told him that?" I asked. She told me she had not. "Well, how's he supposed to know?" She explained that they'd been together for so many years that he should "just know." "No one just knows," I responded. You need to tell him these things. Also, you need to ask him what's important to him. He may have needs you're not meeting as well. After a few weeks when we had dinner with them as a couple, both Paul and Susan thanked me for the conversation I had with Susan. The reason this story is important is because it perfectly illustrates how if this disconnect continued Paul and Susan's relationship could have been susceptible to an affair. Both

Paul and Susan were feeling disconnected; Paul felt unappreciated as did Susan. If either one of them had talked to another person who they felt met their needs better, that's exactly where an affair could have started. Paul and Susan love each other. The problem was they weren't meeting each other's needs. It's very easy to protect your relationship from an affair. Have open and honest conversations about your needs on at least a monthly basis and, if either you or your spouse learn of a problem forming, fix it before it gets worse. Remember, love will get you there, but communication will keep you there.

Cue Card: Create and maintain family traditions with your partner.

One of the best things you can do to strengthen the bond of your marriage is to create family traditions with your partner. A lot of people think you have to have children to create traditions, but that's not true. Regardless of whether or not you have children, when you married your partner the two of you became a family—a new, small family. Traditions don't need to be complicated or expensive, and they don't necessarily always have to fall on holidays. The key factor in creating a tradition is that it should be consistent, and a secondary goal should be to make it enjoyable. Traditions are important because they help give us a sense of shared identity. This is a great thing for a long-term relationship. In addition, traditions give us something to look forward to, and some studies have even shown that traditions help reduce stress. If you are going to have children, or now after marriage have a blended family, think of traditions your kids would enjoy. Engaging in traditions has been linked to increased academic success in children, and other studies have shown that kids who engage in traditions have better social skills. One tradition my husband and I share is that we read to one another on Sunday nights---articles, books—anything either of us finds interesting. Not only have we learned of each other's interests in more detail, but we've also expanded our vocabulary.

Here are some ideas that may help you figure out what traditions may be a good fit for you and your partner:

Take a bike ride to the farmers market every week.

Cook dinner together on Saturdays.

Go for a twenty-minute walk together either before work or after dinner in the evening.

Join a co-ed softball team.

Take a fun class together at a local community college and/or recreation center once or twice a year.

Cue Card: When you disagree, practice the art of maintaining a mutual level of respect with your spouse.

Disagreements and arguments are a part of any marriage. Just because you have them does not mean you have an unhealthy relationship. What makes arguments damaging to your relationship is when they turn ugly. Words can cause deep wounds that sometimes never heal. Therefore, it's important that when you argue you don't let your arguments devolve into insults and character assassination. Stay away from name calling, labeling, and dredging up the past. Practice the art of maintaining a mutual level of respect, staying on topic, and agree to disagree if you can't find a middle ground.

Cue Card: Be a husband in the know and keep an ongoing pulse on your relationship.

It's important to pay attention to the health of your marriage on an ongoing basis and not slip into a pattern of believing your relationship will survive without attention. Check in with your partner from time-to-time and ask her if there's anything she'd like to improve in your relationship. Open up a dialogue with her to see how she feels about things and, in turn, it will give you the opportunity to share where you're at with *your* feelings. If there are any concerns, don't fall into magical thinking and assume that the issues will "just work themselves out." They won't. If either of you have concerns about your relationship, take strides to fix the issues you have. Marital relationships are constantly evolving regardless of how long you've been married. Tune in and pay attention to your relationship, fix the issues that arise, and your marriage will continue to thrive.

Cue Card: Don't share secrets with another woman.

Sharing secrets your wife doesn't know about with another woman is a recipe for disaster. It's important to have friends, and it's totally possible to have friends of both genders, but it's *not* okay to have a closer friendship with another female than the relationship you share with your spouse. (And yes, that goes for online relationships as well.) The reason for this is that when men share a closer relationship with a female other than their wife, it can very quickly spiral into an emotional affair. Play your hand close to your chest and don't put you and your marriage in a vulnerable position by forming a close emotional friendship with a woman other than your spouse. Your marriage will be much less vulnerable to an affair, your wife will be happier, and you'll be happier because you won't be bringing an element of temptation into your marriage. No one likes to be on the "outside" of a secret. When you share secrets and/or intimate details with someone other than your partner, you're basically forming another intimate relationship with an outside person. Be emotionally faithful and ensure this happens by keeping your secrets between you and your partner.

Cue Card: Come to an agreement about the use of porn in your relationship.

Studies show that people who view porn on a regular basis are less satisfied with their lives in general—and that goes for both men *and* women. Science also tells us that there is a direct correlation between use of pornography and sexual intimacy. While there are some couples who enjoy viewing pornography together, I urge you to use caution if this is something you and your wife decide to do. Continually check in with each other to make sure you are on the same page when it comes to your desire to view pornography together. If you don't, over time you may find that one of you may become resentful of your need to view pornography before becoming intimate with one another. It may raise feelings of resentment, jealousy, and possibly feelings of betrayal—none of which are good things for a marriage.

Also, just because it seems to have become more acceptable to some people to view porn today, it doesn't mean you should use that as an excuse to use porn if it's causing a problem in your relationship. If I'm being perfectly honest, I can think of very few women in real life who are okay with their men looking at porn at every opportunity. Yes, some women are more okay with it than others, but what seems to be a bigger issue is if men are sneaky with their porn use. If you want to view porn but she doesn't, have an honest conversation with your partner about your desire to see if you can reach some type of compromise. Come up with what's considered "okay usage" in your relationship and, if you can't agree, then maybe you need to consider if each of you is with the right partner. There is no right or wrong answer when it comes to a topic like this. It is what is right for each individual in the relationship, and what's right for your relationship overall, that should determine the boundaries for porn usage.

Cue Card: Don't hide important things from your wife.

Both you and your wife are entitled to your privacy even when you're married. But if you're hiding something you know she isn't going to like, then you're probably doing something you're not supposed to be doing. As a general rule of thumb, if you think an argument will ensue if your wife finds out, or if it's something you might feel embarrassed about, then there's a very good chance it's something you shouldn't be hiding or, more likely, even doing. Simply put, secrets create distance in relationships.

Cue Card: Housework: It's not just for women.

Your partner is not your mother. It is not her responsibility to pick up after you. When you live with your spouse, it is not the same as living with college roommates or buddies where it is often okay to leave a pizza box on the couch or dirty socks wherever they may land after you take them off. For those of you in relationships where your partner works and you don't, I can't even begin to tell you how important it is that you help out around the house. Practically nothing will help build up resentment in a relationship faster than a spouse who comes home to her husband who doesn't work and finds that he hasn't done any housework (the same is true when the situation is reversed). If you have children, pick up toys so they're not scattered about the house. If you cook during the day, clean the kitchen afterward and put your dirty dishes in the dishwasher. (A lot of enjoyment is taken out of a home cooked meal when you leave your partner the task of cleaning the dishes after you cook. Show her you really care by doing this task yourself.) If you use the bathroom, don't leave it a mess when you're done. Clean up the toothpaste from the sink, close the toilet lid and, if you're feeling like you really want to earn some extra points, squeegee the shower.

Cue Card: Be someone your partner wants to spend time with.

If you have a tendency to be critical of everything your partner does, or come across angry more days than not, it will eventually become hard for your partner to have positive and loving feelings for you. Who wants to be around someone who is always negative or angry? With all of life's challenges, it may be hard not to be negative, but try to remember that you and your partner are a team. Keeping a positive tone to your relationship will help you face life's challenges together with greater resolve and will also increase your romantic feelings toward one another.

Fatherhood

If you and your wife have decided to have children, you will be happy to know that there are many physical and even some psychological benefits for men who have kids. Studies show that men who have children are less likely to have heart problems, less likely to engage in risk-taking behaviors, make better choices in nutrition, feel less depressed, and enjoy overall better health. So even though you may be stressed and overwhelmed with all-things fatherhood, try to hang in there because there seems to be a very positive payoff for men who become fathers. In addition to the health and psychological benefits, you will have the opportunity to see and experience the world through the eyes of your child--what could be more rewarding than that? Below are Cue Cards that will help set you on the right path to be the best dad ever.

Before the Baby Comes

As you and your partner transition into parenthood, use the Cue Cards that follow as stepping stones to help make your path a little easier.

Cue Card: Take a parenting class with your wife.

If you are a first-time father, consider taking a parenting class with your wife. Not only will a parenting class help you understand your role as a parent better, it will also help you gain confidence as a father. You will learn about your forthcoming child's developmental stages, and you will also get a chance to meet other newly expectant fathers and possibly add to your network of friends. In addition to learning something new, you will have the added benefit of doing an activity with your wife that will be a bonding experience. Your participation will also send the message to her that you will be there to support her through her pregnancy and beyond.

Cue Card: Be patient with her mood swings and feelings of fatigue.

As your wife's pregnancy progresses, she may become a little moody and perhaps a little irritable. Depending on the physical symptoms she has related to pregnancy, she also may not feel like doing her normal routine. Be patient. Hormones tend to fluctuate during a pregnancy, and this could cause her to have mood swings and physical symptoms she doesn't normally have. Some days she just may not feel like doing anything because her back hurts or her feet are swollen.

Do a little extra work around the house; ask her if there's anything she needs and try not to react in anger or frustration if she is moody. She'll appreciate it, and even if she tries your patience, think of the things you do for her during this time as just more ways to show her through your actions that you love and care for her. Trust me—you would much rather have her remember you as being kind and understanding during her pregnancy as opposed to impatient and unforgiving.

Cue Card: Help your wife feel comfortable and secure while she gives birth.

Help alleviate a tremendous amount of stress for your partner when she gives birth by making sure her needs and desires are met while she is in the hospital. Some women have no issue with—and actually enjoy—family members being present during the birthing process, while others prefer to keep it a private experience. There are no right or wrong answers other than the only right answer is what your wife wants. If she only wants you present, or perhaps her mother present, then these are the wishes that should be honored, and it will be *your* responsibility to make sure things happen the way she wants them to since she won't be in a position to enforce any boundaries she would like in place. You may have to tell some very enthusiastic family members who desire to be present that they are not welcome, and while they may be angry with you and your partner about the situation, they will simply need to get over it. The birth of your child is a crucial time for you to be there for your wife and stand up for her since she can't do it for herself. Show her you're dependable and that you are looking out for her best interests by giving and doing the things she needs.

As Your Children Grow

Fatherhood isn't limited to conceiving a child--it's a lifetime event. The Cue Cards below will help you be a great father for your children at every stage of their lives.

Cue Card: Be a good role model for your children.

If you want your children to grow up to be responsible adults who love and support their families, have good jobs, and lead good lives, you will need to live your life in a similar manner. Parents are the primary role models for their children, and it is unrealistic to expect your child to grow into a responsible adult if you're not one yourself.

Are you materialistic? Do you throw a temper tantrum when you don't get your way? Do you treat others poorly? Do you have a problem controlling your alcohol intake? If your answer is yes to any of these questions, I can just about assure you that your child will display the same behaviors you do when he or she grows older. Take pride in what you do for a living, treat your wife right, and strive to live with integrity, and your children will most likely grow up to do the same.

Cue Card: Present a united front as parents.

Regardless of what differences you have with your partner, you should always present as a united front to your children. If you and your partner disagree on parenting issues, talk with each other in private. Seek to find an agreement or, at the very least, a compromise for common ground when it comes to things such as discipline, school performance, homework habits, chores, general behavior, and conduct. When you present as a united front, both of you will send a more consistent message to your child about expectations and discipline. In turn, when your child grows older, a united front will reduce the possibility that your child will try to pit one of you against the other when trying to get his or her way. Also, parents who present a united front send the message that you and your partner are in control and back each other up, which is another great way to role model good relationship and parenting skills to your child.

Cue Card: Spend time with your kids.

Fathers add so much to the lives of their children, so don't ever underestimate your role in your child's life or think that your child's mother can pick up the slack for you. (Most women find men who spend time with their kids more attractive too--so this will help you in the romance department as well.) Children who have their fathers involved in their lives have higher levels of self-esteem, do better at school, and are more successful in their work relationships in later life. So, when you think your kids don't really need you, think again--they do.

Cue Card: Encourage your children's strengths.

It's a very normal feeling to want your kids to be "just like you," but keep in mind that your children *aren't* you. They may have very different personalities, dispositions, and strengths. It's a little unrealistic to expect an introverted child who seems to prefer doing solitary activities such as reading or drawing to want to be a pop star or politician. Conversely, it's unrealistic to expect a very outgoing child who seems to thrive in working with others to become a research scientist. Encourage your child's individuality and their strengths and your children will flourish. For a real-life example, I will share with you this: I was always an introverted child who enjoyed writing and creating art. Although I enjoyed some sports, I was never really good at any of them. If my parents would have pushed me to be a professional athlete of some type, they would have been sorely disappointed. I would not have succeeded in the world of professional sports and, during it all, I most likely would have been miserable. Also, if they had insisted on denying my strengths, there would have been a very good chance that I would have never written the book you are reading today.

Cue Card: Be involved with their schooling.

Studies show us that when fathers are involved in the schooling of their children, children have better peer relationships, higher levels of self-esteem, and do better at school. I'm not saying you have to attend every PTA meeting and bake sale but try to make as many school events as you are able to for the sake of your children. When you're active and involved in your child's schooling, you send the message through your actions that education is important. This is far more effective than any long-winded lecture would ever be.

Here are some unique ways you can become more involved:

1. Offer to create and maintain a monthly newsletter for your child's class or school.

2. Arrange a field trip for your child's class to your workplace.

3. Help your child with homework assignments once a week.

4. Create a website for your child's school or class.

5. Help your child's school arrange a "Bring your Dad to School" night or a father/daughter dance night.

Cue Card: Have dinner as a family.

Try to have dinner as a family as often as you can. (I recommend at least four times a week.) Children who eat dinner with their families tend to develop better social skills that they will be able to use in other areas of their lives such as at school and, when they get older, in the workplace. In addition, studies show that children who eat dinner with their families on a regular basis are less likely to have issues with alcohol and substance abuse as they get older, and they are also less inclined to develop eating disorders.

If you have difficulty finding time to eat with your children, consider reframing the idea of dining together as an investment in their future. Good social skills are invaluable in all relationships. By simply eating dinner with your children on a regular basis, you can teach them how to interact with others in a respectful manner. When you dine together as a family, you will also have the opportunity to monitor your child in a way that isn't obvious to them when you're engaging in pleasant conversation on a regular basis. You will be able to see if your child seems a little more moody than normal, or perhaps troubled in some other manner which will give you the chance to help or intervene before a possible problem escalates out of control.

Cue Card: Be consistent with your discipline.

One of the most important aspects of parenting is discipline. The second most important aspect is that the discipline you give your children is consistent. Children who receive consistent discipline from their parents develop a sense of security and a good sense of boundaries which could reduce the possibility of emotional difficulties down the road. Disciplining your child with consistency shows your children that you care for them, and it teaches them self-control—a valuable skill that they will be able to use for the rest of their lives. There is an art to discipline: too much discipline may result in your child rebelling as he or she gets older, and too little discipline may yield the same result. The key is to come to an agreement with your spouse about what the rules will be and what form of discipline will be received if rules are broken. Remember, don't be heavy handed; consistency is always more important and effective because it teaches children that there are no exceptions when rules are made and it sets a minimum expectation for their behavior.

Cue Card: Always treat the mother of your children with respect.

Don't berate your partner or make negative comments about her parenting style in front of your children. Your children look to you as a role model and will learn behaviors and attitudes from you. It's a little unrealistic to think that your kids will treat their mom respectfully if you don't. In addition, if you have a daughter, she will learn it is okay for her eventual life partner to treat her disrespectfully because this is what you will be teaching her. If you have a son, you can bet he will treat any partner he has with disrespect because his dad (meaning you) raised him to see this type of behavior as acceptable.

Chapter Five

Cue Cards for Sex

Studies indicate that men who have sex at least once a week lower their risk of a heart attack by thirty percent, their risk of stroke by fifty percent, and their risk of diabetes by forty percent. In addition, men who enjoy active sex lives are more likely to live longer too. Here is another interesting fact for you: Endorphins released during sexual activity create a euphoria similar to that produced by opioid drug use--these same endorphins also act as extremely effective pain killers.

All of that sounds pretty good, doesn't it?

Obviously, there are many positive things to be derived from having a good sex life, and in this chapter that's what we're going to cover. The first part of this chapter will be devoted to how to increase your chances of having more sex; the second part will talk about how to have great sex; and the chapter will end with some Cue Cards to help you extend your sex life well into old age.

How to Have More Sex

Let the Cue Cards that follow help increase your odds of having more sex on a regular basis.

Cue Card: Sex begins way before the bedroom; so help her feel sexy and connected to you as much as possible.

You won't believe the amount of men who come to my therapy office telling me their wives are not interested in sex. Actually, this is probably the number one complaint I get

57

from men who are in long-term relationships. Inevitably, when I do some investigating about why wives feel turned off to their husbands, the majority of women tell me something to the effect of "the only time he's nice to me or pays attention to me is when he wants sex."

This may surprise you, but did you know when you have sex with us that you're usually having it with us 24 hours a day? It's true. We feel more sexual with you and toward you when we feel like you are connected to us at times that aren't related to foreplay. Were you nice to our mom? Did you surprise us and cook dinner with the kids one night when we came home from work? Did you actually fold the laundry? Did you say we looked great in that outfit?

If you're consistently sweet and kind to us, we'll be more drawn to you. In short, when you're into *us*, we are into *you*. And being into us does not always mean sexually—it means you are aware of the things that are important to us and that you're there for us when we need you.

If you want to have more sex in your relationship, you will have to pay attention to your partner long before you approach her for sex. I'm not saying you have to fawn over her every minute, but it's important to pay attention and to comment on the little things you notice. Does her hair look great? Has she lost weight? Is she great with the kids? Has she given you good advice? Tell her!

The other important thing to do is to engage in non-sexual activities on a regular basis. I recommend at least three times a week. Go to the movies, cook a meal together, play board games, or go for walks or bike rides together. I understand for many (myself included) that this is sometimes difficult to work into your schedule but remember the non-sexual activities you do don't need to be expensive or complicated. The simple goal is to connect with each other in a way that is non-sexual. Most women like to feel bonded with their partners on multiple levels, not just in a sexual way and when you do non-sexual activities with your partner. It helps foster additional levels of connection. Make your sex life hotter by doing non-sexual things with your partner before you make a move toward the bedroom. Both of you will be much happier with the end result.

Cue Card: Learn what turns her on.

Some women like to be romanced and have a lot of foreplay, while others may prefer to sneak in a quickie from time-to-time. Your partner will be more inclined to have sex with you often if you learn what she likes when you make love. The thinking behind this is very simple: it's very attractive to us when a man gives us what we want and it makes us want more. Your partner will want more of *you* if you give her what she wants in bed. Be inquisitive and be unique and, most likely, she will find you irresistible.

Cue Card: Approach when the time is right.

Women don't have an on/off switch when it comes to emotions. So, if you're going to approach your partner for sex, you'd hedge your bet if you approached her when she's in a good place emotionally. Stress can kill just about anyone's libido. If you see your partner running stressed, figure out what you can do to help. This will help you in the romance department. If she's upset about something like a bad day at the office, or problems with the kids, talk with her and let her vent her frustrations. If there's anything you can do to help her manage her stress better, do it. This will help her feel more relaxed and more connected to you.

Cue Card: Teach her about what turns you on.

Most women love to please their partner sexually—it's a turn on for us. You may have great chemistry with a woman, but she'll never know everything you like sexually until you *let* her know. Never assume she'll be able to figure it out on her own. While she may in time be able to figure it out, think of how much of a better time you'd be having if she knew it all sooner. Speak up and let her know. She'll be appreciative and be a better lover when you do.

How to Have Great Sex

The Cue Cards that follow will help you take your skills as a lover from good to great.

Cue Card: Be a generous lover.

There are few things less appealing to women than men who don't reciprocate sexually. The best sex is mutually satisfying. If you're taking more than you're giving, it's time to equal things out. Women love men who are unselfish in bed.

Cue Card: Toys aren't necessarily just for children.

Don't be afraid to integrate sex toys into your sex life. More women use them than you probably are aware of. A recent study indicates that 51% of women use them with the most common toy being a vibrator. Women don't view toys as a replacement for your time together; they view it as an enhancement; so never feel intimidated by a device. If you can adopt a more playful attitude toward sex, it can help you have a more adventurous and fun sex life.

Cue Card: Sleep Naked.

Studies show that couples who sleep naked together have more sex. Another added benefit of sleeping naked together is it helps facilitate a stronger bond between couples. Sex aside, did you know there are actual health benefits to sleeping together in the nude? Sleeping naked facilitates skin-to-skin contact which, in turn, facilitates the stimulation of the hormone oxytocin. Oxytocin has all kinds of feel-good benefits that include a decreased heart-rate, a reduction in stress, and increased feelings of sexual arousal. Encourage her or share this cue card with her to help her learn the benefits of sleeping in the nude with you.

Cue Card: Cuddle Afterward.

I realize a lot of you reading this will roll your eyes when you read this Cue Card, but the truth of the matter is there are few things that are more distancing to us women than a man who ignores us after we have sex with him. You may be done with us at this point, but after sex we are *not* done with you. Cuddling after sex helps us feel closer to you. Also when you cuddle with us instead of reaching for your smart phone, cigarette, or television remote, we'll be that much more inclined to have sex with you the next time you ask, because we'll also look forward to the time we get to share with you afterward.

Cue Card: Have sex in unique places.

Having sex in unexpected places is a fantasy for many women (as well as men). Off of a hiking trail perhaps? Maybe behind a sand dune at the beach, or even in a secluded spot off a winding country road? Most of us love this type of thing because the spontaneity of it makes us feel desired. There's also a slight thrill of knowing you're doing something in a place you *may* get caught. Be careful though and *don't* get caught—just be discreet and have fun!

Sex After Forty

Don't let age get you down—literally and figuratively. These Cue Cards will help you continue to have good sex well into old age.

Cue Card: Shed a little light on the situation and have sex in the morning.

As we get older, it's quite natural for men and women to have less energy as the day progresses. Consider having sex in the morning when you and your body are more awake. The added benefit to having daytime sex is you'll be able to see more too—a little visual stimulation always seems to help.

Cue Card: Don't be embarrassed by needing a little extra help.

Every woman knows that as men age their erections are not as spontaneous, nor are they as firm as they used to be. If you're struggling with the fact that you need a little extra time and energy to achieve an erection, don't be embarrassed to talk about it. If you don't express how you're feeling, your performance anxiety could get the best of you and possibly make your situation worse than it needs to be. When you're forthcoming about any difficulty you are having, your partner will most likely be more supportive than you think. As women, we like to help those that are close to us and helping out in a sexual situation is no different. Speak up and let us help you—we like that type of thing.

Cue Card: There's more to sex than just intercourse.

There is no rule that states that sex has to include intercourse. In fact, there are a variety of ways to enjoy sexual intimacy without penetration. Here are some ideas to get you started:

Practice erotic touch and let your hands sensuously explore each other's bodies.

Kiss passionately.

Have oral sex.

Write down the erotic fantasies you have of your partner and share them with each other—words can be a very strong aphrodisiac.

Chapter Six

Cue Cards for Your Health

You probably don't pay too much attention to your health (most men don't), but in this chapter I'm going to talk about why you should. I recently read a study that said many men between the ages of 18 to 50 don't have a primary care physician. Given that fact, is it really a surprise that women tend to outlive men by five to ten years? Perhaps if men took more interest in their healthcare, this number would even out. No one is really sure why men don't seem to take an interest in their health much until something goes wrong, but some theories seem to suggest that it may be because when men are younger they're reared toward "toughing it out" and "getting though the pain," you know--the whole no pain, no gain concept.

If this describes you, I urge you to cast this mindset aside and at least take a *little* bit of interest in your health regardless of how young you may be and what great physical condition you may be in. Health is something you should never take chances with. Will it really kill you to get a physical once a year? No, it won't--but if you don't, your choice of *not* getting a physical every year may. Many ailments and conditions don't have any symptoms until they are well advanced, and when you go for a yearly physical exam, if anything is wrong it can be detected early and, in many cases, fixed. It's very easy to take good health for granted but, believe me, you will miss your good health status if you no longer have it. You invest time and energy into all other aspects of your life--your education, your career, your friends, your family, and your relationship, why not take sixty minutes once a year and go see your physician for a complete physical? It's the best investment you can make in yourself and for those who care about you. That said, the Cue Cards in this chapter were created to help keep you in the best physical condition possible.

Take Control of Your Health

Many people take better care of their cars than they do of their health. Don't be one of these people. While it's true some people are blessed with good health, even the healthiest of people may run into issues with illness or disabilities at one point or another in their lives. Don't take an auto-pilot approach to your health—be proactive by implementing the Cue Cards that follow.

Cue Card: Know your health risk factors.

Genetics can play a significant factor in your health. Do you know *your* genetic risk factors? If not, you should. You can start taking strides to reduce your risk of some hereditary diseases by educating yourself on preventative measures and informing your doctor of your concerns so he knows what types of screening tests he should consider conducting during your yearly exams. In my family, diabetes and heart disease seem to run through our family tree; therefore, I take steps to mitigate these risk factors by getting routine blood tests, eating a healthy diet, and exercising. To date, I haven't been diagnosed with heart disease or diabetes. In fact, out of my immediate family, I am the only one who is not on blood pressure medication. I attribute much of my good health to knowing what could be ahead of me if I don't watch it. If you know your risks factors, *you* can take similar steps and hopefully have the same result and remain disease free.

Cue Card: Schedule an appointment with your physician.

As I mentioned in the introduction of this chapter, there are many health conditions that don't have any symptoms until they are well advanced. At a yearly physical examination, your physician can order screening tests for things such as diabetes, cancer, and heart disease, as well as various orthopedic issues. Your physician will also do a prostate exam. When health issues are caught and treated early, some can be reversed and others can be treated which will help you enjoy a good quality of life for many years to come. No one chooses to be sick or not feel well, but if you don't get a yearly exam, you may be robbing yourself of future good health—which could lead to depression. Why cheat yourself out of a healthy life when you don't have to?

Help your physician take better care of you by providing him with as much information about your health history as possible. Include as much information about your family of origin's health as you possibly can and be sure to inform your doctor about any medications and supplements you take. Don't listen to others who tell you "you don't need a physical, you look fine." Listen to me—you *do*, and if you don't do it for yourself, do it for your partner and your children because they need you too.

Cue Card: If you are prescribed medication, take it as you're instructed to.

If your physician prescribes a medication for you, you will get much more out of it if you take it the way it's prescribed (e.g., with meals, in the morning, etc.), and for the duration it's prescribed for. Many people stop taking medication when they feel better, but this usually isn't a good idea. People seem to forget that the reason they are in fact feeling better is because they *are* taking their medication. If you have questions about discontinuing your medication, always check with your physician first.

Cue Card: Follow your physician's advice.

If you physician tells you to lose weight and exercise, try to do these things. If your physician wants to see you for a follow-up appointment in three months, schedule it. If your physician recommends additional tests, get them. Doctors don't make things up because they've got nothing better to do—they make recommendations about your health because they *want* you to be healthy.

General Well-being

There are a number of simple things you can do each day that may have an enormous impact on your general well-being. I've created the Cue Cards below to help you take better care of yourself.

Cue Card: Eat right.

Men generally have an easier time losing weight than women do, but even if you don't have a weight problem, you should try to maintain a healthy diet and limit your intake of fast food. You may have a lean, muscular physique and think that you can eat whatever and as much as you want, but eventually--even if you're in great shape presently—your poor eating habits *will* catch up with you. Poor eating habits lead to a myriad of health issues including obesity, heart disease, diabetes, and some studies even suggest that an unhealthy diet could increase your risk of certain cancers. Of course, it's okay to indulge every once in a while but strive to not make a pattern of your indulgences, or eventually you will most likely see it in your waistline.

Cue Card: Get adequate rest.

You will be better at everything you do during the day if you get a good night's sleep on a regular basis (most studies suggest a minimum of 7.5 hours each night). Sleep will help you handle stress better, will help keep you healthy, and even help you handle your relationship better. Let's face it, when we're running sleep deprived, most of us eventually get a little edgy--being even just a *little* edgy never helps a relationship. You'll be happier if your relationship is happier, so don't skimp on sleep. If you have problems falling asleep, consider trying the following things to help you meet the sandman in short order:

Limit your caffeine intake and stop drinking caffeinated beverages by early afternoon.

Stop using electronic devices such as tablets and smartphones at least two hours before bedtime, as some studies suggest that the blue hue of the light emanating from electronic devices may interfere with your serotonin level (serotonin is a hormone you need for sleep).

Sleep in a dark room.

Limit your alcohol intake—contrary to popular belief, alcohol does *not* help sleep.

Try to go to sleep the same time every night and get up around the same time each day.

Exercise, but not too close to bedtime. Stress is often a sleep thief and exercising on a regular basis will help reduce your stress levels. You don't need to strive for six-pack-abs, but most studies suggest you should aim for at least thirty minutes of cardiovascular exercise a day, at least five days a week. You'll feel better and age better if you do.

Cue Card: Don't smoke.

Smoking can lead to a myriad of health issues. Men who smoke tobacco have a 23% higher chance of contracting lung cancer, are more likely to have sleep difficulties, have acid reflux, and to incur skin damage that results in an older looking appearance. In addition, men who smoke have a lower sperm count and are less responsive to fertility treatments. One fact that doesn't seem to be highly publicized is that smoking damages your vascular system which eventually will lead to difficulties maintaining an erection. If you do smoke, I encourage you to stop as soon as possible. If you struggle with stopping, consider visiting your physician to explore what type of medications and treatment options may be available to you to help curb your cravings.

Cue Card: Don't use and/or abuse substances.

Nothing good comes from substance abuse—it's hard on your body, it's hard on your mental health, it's hard on the people you share relationships with, and it won't help you in your career. Inevitably, there will be some of you reading this thinking, "I can handle my drugs," and I'm going to tell you why you are wrong in your belief—drug use impairs your judgment. Just because you haven't had any problems yet doesn't mean it will always be that way. One of the biggest issues with substance abuse is that all it takes is one mishap—one accident, one blackout, one arrest for driving under the influence, one incident of erratic behavior—and you're whole career and life could be changed in an instant (and you could accidently kill someone while driving impaired). Play it on the safe side and refrain from using and abusing substances—that includes abusing prescription medication as well.

Cue Card: Manage your stress.

Stress can wreak havoc not only on your emotional well-being but on your physical health as well. It can make you feel irritable, anxious, depressed, and physically stress can cause you to have aches and pains, heartburn, constipation, diarrhea, and high blood pressure which eventually could lead to a stroke or heart attack. There have also been some recent studies that link high levels of stress to elevated rates of inflammation in the body. Inflammation is no one's friend and is associated with many chronic diseases. Don't take chances with your stress level because, as tough as you may think you are, stress can kill you if you don't keep it under control.

Here are five quick stress reduction techniques you can start practicing today:

1) Spend some time with your friends. Go shoot hoops, go surfing, or just hang out—it will help you unwind.

2) Get a massage.

3) Practice deep breathing. Sit in your chair with your feet on the floor, close your eyes, take deep breaths, and exhale slowly for five minutes a few times each day.

4) Actually, *take* your lunch break. Take thirty minutes out of your mid-day schedule, turn off your phone, and either go have lunch somewhere away from your workplace or go for a walk.

5) Have sex. Who said stress reduction can't be fun? Have you ever met anyone who was still stressed after passionate sex? I didn't think so.

Cue Card: Help maintain good overall physical health by staying on top of your oral health.

Oral health and dental hygiene are very important to your overall health, so if you haven't seen the dentist in over a year, it's time to make an appointment for a cleaning and for an exam. Some studies indicate that oral health plays a role in cardiovascular disease, diabetes, and a few other diseases as well—including Alzheimer's disease. Also, if you're consistent in your dental care, you may end up avoiding costly dental bills down the road, because your dentist will be able to catch small issues such as cavities and gum disease early before they require extensive and costly treatments.

Cue Card: Stay socially active.

Men tend to be less social than women, but science shows that regardless of gender, staying socially active in real life has many benefits (social media, gaming, and online friends don't count). Studies show that when people are socially active, they have lower blood pressure, lower heart rates, and they even catch fewer colds than people who have a tendency to isolate. For those of you reading this who are married, congratulations—statistics show that marriage will add years to your life. If you find yourself alone most nights of the week, take strides to improve your in-person social network. Join a gym or a class—anything that's not online. There are many ways to meet people, but you have to put yourself in the position to be able to do it. Trust me, a few hours away from your electronic device won't kill you. In fact, it will most likely be one of the best things you can do for yourself. Step away from the computer, turn off the television, and look for opportunities to meet people in person and create real-life friendships as this will be one of the best steps you will take in achieving optimum health.

Health After the Age of 40

If you've taken care of your health most of your life, there's a good chance that most of you will be in pretty good shape by the time you reach the age of forty. Can people after the age of 40 continue to enjoy great health? Of course, they can. Let the Cue Cards in this section help you experience optimal health beyond the age of 50.

Cue Card: Keep your future in focus by getting a yearly eye exam.

One of the first senses affected by aging is vision. While you age, it's relatively common to experience changes in your vision, but you will be able to preserve your eyesight longer and possibly prevent vision loss from aging related eye diseases by visiting an optometrist, or ophthalmologist once a year for an eye exam. A yearly eye exam helps spot problems, and during your visit your eye doctor can monitor your vision and suggest corrective action—either glasses, contact lenses, or even laser surgery to help you see better. Your physician may even have dietary tips and supplement suggestions that will help you maintain good vision as long as possible.

Cue Card: Ask your physician to check your hormone levels.

Science indicates that testosterone levels in men decrease at the rate of about one percent a year after the age of 30. You probably won't notice the drop that much at first, but if you do the math, by the time you're 70 your testosterone levels will be a whopping fifty percent less than they were in your 30s. The decrease in testosterone can lead to muscle loss, changes in mood and cognition, problems with sleep, a lower libido, and erectile dysfunction. Your doctor will be able to determine your hormone levels with a simple blood test and can suggest treatment options that may be able to help alleviate and/or minimize any symptoms you may have.

Cue Card: Keep going strong by staying physically active.

Your back may hurt and your joints may feel a little more achy than they used to, but don't let that stop you from participating in regular exercise (with your physician's approval, of course). Staying physically active on a regular basis can actually help relieve some of the symptoms related to joint pain and keep you from feeling stiff. In addition, regular physical activity can help combat aging related weight gain and muscle loss.

Cue Card: Help sharpen your listening skills by getting a hearing examination.

Hearing loss is more common in men than it is in women, so it's always a good idea to get a hearing exam on a yearly basis. Age related hearing loss occurs gradually, and it's caused when the tiny hair cells in the inner ear that convert sound energy into electrical impulses to the brain deteriorate. A licensed audiologist can help you preserve your ability to hear and provide you with assistive devices if and when needed. If you do end up needing a hearing device, don't think for a minute you'll be wearing that ugly thing your grandfather had on his ear—many devices are barely noticeable today. The other benefit of keeping your hearing intact is this: you will give others one less reason to yell at you.

Chapter Seven

Cue Cards for Divorce

If you've read the first few chapters of this book, you've learned the skills needed to help make your marriage last forever, but what happens if your partner decides she wants a divorce? It's not unusual for women to initiate divorce proceedings--in fact, some studies show that women initiate 75 percent of all divorces. As much as I don't like the topic or thought of divorce, and as much as I encourage couples to work through their difficulties and stay together, it would be remiss of me not to talk about divorce in this book. Men seem to have so few resources when it comes to this topic, and many men often tell me that they feel that "the system is against them." While I'm not an attorney and don't know much about legal proceedings when it comes to divorce, this chapter will be able to help you with "the rest of the stuff" men don't typically seem to get a lot of help or support with when their marriage ends.

If you're reading this and are currently going through a divorce, please know that your feelings of sadness and loss are very normal. Men on the whole get more depressed after a divorce than women do partly because women tend to emotionally process a divorce before they initiate it and also because, quite honestly, for men divorce usually entails quite a bit more loss than it does for women. There's the loss of seeing kids every day, the loss of income due to child and spousal support, and because men tend to be less social with peer networking than women are, there's definitely a social loss when a marriage ends. When all is said and done, men are left feeling very isolated. Because it's often viewed as "not manly" for men to talk about being lonely and feeling isolated, a lot of men just kind of repress their feelings and suffer in silence. But now that you have my book and are reading this chapter, I'm going to help you work through your feelings and help get your life back on track post-divorce.

This chapter will start with how to get through the initial phases of divorce, then we'll talk about how to keep yourself together during the divorce proceedings, and end with steps you can take to help rebuild your life after your divorce is final.

When a Divorce is Imminent

As mentioned, women initiate most of the divorces but, as you know, *most* does not equal *always*. Below, we'll look at Cue Cards that will help guide you through the initial phases of a divorce and how to let the people you care about know about the impending change in your marital status.

Cue Card: If you're going to ask your wife for a divorce, be gentle, be kind, and be direct.

There is never a good time to ask someone for a divorce, nor is there ever an easy way to do it. If you've reached a point where your marriage is no longer workable, while it may not come as a huge surprise to your spouse that you are asking for a divorce, it still will most likely be quite difficult for her to hear. Try to find a time and a place to discuss your intent to divorce that is calm and away from others in the event your exchange gets heated. Asking for a divorce can bring up a lot of emotions to the forefront for both of you, so you will want to minimize the possibility of bringing others into your conversation who may be impacted by what is going on between the two of you (e.g., your children), or perhaps others who may "take sides" and make an already volatile situation even more so.

Try as hard you can to be as kind as possible but be direct and do not leave a door open for reconciliation if it's not possible for there to be one. Offering false hope never works and will only make further discussions about the dissolution of your marriage more difficult. Strive to understand that your wife will be upset, and most likely she'll either be very sad, very angry, or perhaps a combination of both of these emotions and may say or react to your information negatively. Be ready to handle her emotions and not run from them or get angry at her for having them. Remember, the end of your marriage will bring up all kinds of feelings for both of you—sadness, anger, resentment—again, all of these feelings are normal. When a marriage ends, many people feel a tremendous sense of loss because it *is* a loss—it's a loss of hope, a loss of a dream, and a loss of a future. That said, you still need to do what you need to do and, if you are going to ask for a divorce, be respectful and as caring as you can be. No one likes to hurt another person; don't forget, this is the woman you once vowed to spend the rest of your life with. If you must break that vow, realize you are talking to the woman you once felt you could never live without and try to state your feelings from that perspective. Of course, what you plan to say to her is hurtful, but it will be less hurtful if you do it in as much of a loving way as possible.

Here is an example you can use to help you formulate your own words...

I am sorry that our lives have brought us to this point, and I hope you know that I would never purposely hurt you, but I need to ask you for a divorce.

The key in a painful situation like this is to stay away from making inflammatory comments, placing blame, and sticking to *I* statements. Of course, your wife will probably still be very hurt and react with anger, blame, and sadness, but if you stay respectful, focused, and caring, you will help to keep this very difficult discussion from becoming a more heated exchange than it needs to be. While you cannot control *her* reaction, you can control what *you* do to feed her reaction, so choose your words wisely.

Cue Card: If your wife tells you she would like to divorce, try not to react in a way that will cause more damage to you and to those around you.

If your wife asks you for a divorce, try as much as possible to listen to what she says to you and understand that it's most likely as difficult for her to tell you she wants to end your marriage as it is for you to hear it. Of course, you will likely feel anger, sadness, resentment, and loneliness, but seek constructive ways to deal with the feelings you have rather than lashing out in anger and/or bringing harm to yourself or others emotionally and physically. Know that it's okay to express your feelings to your wife, and that it's perfectly acceptable to cry—in fact, it's *good* to cry as it will help you work through your emotions much better than holding them in. Here are some things you can try that may help you during this difficult time:

Reach out and spend time with your friends and extended family members. While isolating yourself may sound appealing, it's not one of the more emotionally healthy ways to start healing. Spending time with others who care about you can help lift your spirits and help remind you that even though you may feel lonely, you are not alone.

Get enough rest. Sleep may be difficult during this time, but sleep when you are able to as it will help you feel less "on edge," and adequate rest will also help keep your mind in a place where you can focus on all that will need to be taken care of as your life transitions to its next stage.

Stay away from alcohol and drugs. Though they may be tempting options to help you escape or take a break from your feelings, ultimately, they will not help you and could possibly make matters worse. The *last* thing you need during a difficult time is for your judgment to be impaired or your inhibitions to be lowered to a point where you do something you may regret later.

Cue Card: Inform your children of your divorce in a way that lets them know that they are not at fault for the end of your marriage.

If you have children with your spouse, it's important that you tell them of your decision to divorce. No matter how much ill will exists between you and your soon-to-be ex-partner, remember that both of you will always have a responsibility to be good parents to your children. With that fact in mind, it's best for the kids if you and your spouse can inform your children of your decision to divorce *together*. A lot of children fear they'll never see one parent again after a divorce and telling your children of your divorce together will help minimize (although not eliminate) some of these fears. When you present the information with your spouse, your children will be able to see that you are still on speaking terms and behaving civilly toward one another.

If possible, try to pick a time and day when everyone—you, your spouse and your children—are in a good frame-of-mind as it will help everyone discuss and handle the news better. Keep in mind stress impacts our reactions, so it's always best to try to minimize the stress we're feeling before entering into emotionally charged conversations.

Cue Card: Let extended family members, friends, and colleagues know of your divorce in a way that doesn't present you and your spouse in a bad light.

There's no rule or etiquette guideline that lets us know when the "right" time is to let others outside our immediate family know of our divorce, so you just have to do it at a time that feels right for you and your partner. Ideally, the two of you will be able to come to an agreement together as to when and how you will let others know, but if you can't, use your judgment about what feels instinctually right to you. One thing that you should keep in mind is that speculation is often very hurtful and incorrect, so if you don't want gossip spreading about the state of your marriage, you would do best to control the information train so to speak, and let others know of your decision directly from you.

When you do decide to let the other people in your life know of your divorce, make every attempt to let them know in a way that doesn't place you or your former partner in a negative light. Avoid giving too many details, placing blame, or general badmouthing your partner. No one needs to know the intimate details of the demise of your marriage because it's really no one else's business. Also, when you decide to share information with someone else, you never know who *they* are going to tell your information to, so play it safe and keep your very personal information to yourself as much as possible. The last thing you need at this point in your life is stress from others gossiping about you and your family, so take strides to eliminate their possibilities to do so.

During Your Divorce

Divorce proceedings can take at least six months to complete. During this transitional period of your life, you'll experience a number of emotions and usually question yourself from time-to-time about whether or not you made the right decision. This is all very normal as well. If you have children, this will also be a period of transition for them, and it will be your role to help them learn their "new normal" as their parents move to separate households.

The Cue Cards that follow will help you sort through this complex period with greater ease.

Cue Card: Don't get self-destructive and remember it's okay to ask for help if you need it.

If you feel you're taking your divorce harder than other men going through a similar situation, rest assured, you're not. Studies repeatedly show that it's not uncommon for men to take divorce harder than women. The reason for this is, as I mentioned at the start of this chapter, is that men are often blindsided when their wives ask for a divorce. So, while it may seem as though your former spouse is faring better emotionally, usually the only difference is that she went through what you're currently going through before she asked you for a divorce. She's further along in the grieving cycle, so to speak. Also, even though there haven't been studies on this, I personally believe that men aren't encouraged to talk about their feelings of sadness and frustration as women are encouraged to do while they are going through a divorce.

If you're struggling emotionally getting over your divorce, it's okay for you to get assistance to help process those feelings. If you don't feel like talking to your friends or family, schedule a confidential appointment with a licensed therapist, clergy person, or consider joining a support group of newly divorced men. If you're uncomfortable talking to a woman about your feelings, there are plenty of men who are licensed therapists as well. Please see the resource section at the end of this book for a list of therapist referral websites to help you find the counselor who is right for you.

Cue Card: Try to manage your feelings and don't make your ex-wife's life miserable.

Depending on the circumstances of your divorce, it's understandable that you will most likely feel hurt and perhaps even angry. What's not understandable (and could even be illegal) is leaving a wake of destruction in your path. Don't track down your former wife's new boyfriend, don't drive to her home and destroy her things, don't take out loans in her name, don't run up the credit cards, and don't drain all the back accounts. Nothing ever good comes from being destructive. Both you and your ex-wife are responsible for your debts, and even if you've divided your assets and are legally separated, you could go to jail for taking out loans in her name. Find a more productive way to process your anger--go to the gym or join a sports league with your buddies. Try as hard as you can to stay away from personally and financially self-destructing...in six months to a year you'll be thankful you found a healthier way to channel your anger.

Cue Card: Don't put your kids in the middle of any battles between you and your former spouse.

One of the worst things men (or women for that matter) can do during a divorce is to put their children in the middle of their disagreements. Your children are processing their own emotions during a divorce and, when couples start to play custody games, it's extremely difficult emotionally for them. Your kids love you as their father and they also love their mother--do not make them choose one of you over the other and take sides.

Cue Card: Do not bad mouth your soon-to-be former spouse.

Regardless of what your relationship was like, it's usually a good idea to *not* bad mouth your former spouse to anyone now or even in the future. Of course, you will have ill will--I know of very few couples who have fond things to say of each other post-divorce but, in general, not much good comes from airing your dirty laundry to others.

Looking forward to when you start dating again, keep in mind that if your date is wise, she will form an impression of you based on what you say about your ex-wife. On the flip side, if you're with a woman who wants you to hate your ex-wife, then you may want to pause and consider if this is a woman you really want to be with. Generally speaking, if a woman would want you to speak ill of your ex-wife, she is most likely at least a little insecure. Also take into consideration that you will not want anyone you date to start encouraging your children to speak poorly of your ex-wife, because this would put your children in the middle of a situation that they really have no business being a part of.

Cue Card: Pay your child support as you are instructed to.

If you have children with someone and it doesn't work out, as the father of those children it is your responsibility to make payments toward their care. Did you know if you are not current on your child support payment that you can't get a passport? It's true. The law takes missed child support payments very seriously--as well they should. Your children did not ask to be born into this world, and they are not capable of providing for themselves until they reach adulthood. It is unfair of you to expect your ex to have the sole financial responsibility of caring for your children (and, as mentioned, it's illegal). Don't play games with this issue because, in the end, it's only your children who will suffer. Ask yourself if you want your kids to think of you as a deadbeat dad. If not, pay your child support when it's due and in the amount that's due.

Cue Card: Tie up loose ends and complete your divorce.

Once you've made the decision to divorce and followed through with all of the arduous paperwork, do take the steps necessary to make sure your divorce is finalized. So much time seems to pass between the initial filing of a divorce and the finalization of it that it's not unusual for couples to never officially complete their divorce. While it's certainly understandable why you would not want to give your divorce any more thought, I assure you that you will eventually run into a problem when you meet someone, get serious with her, and tell her "I still have to file a few more papers to get my divorce finalized." Also remember that until your divorce is legally complete, you are technically still married. As much as we seem to live in an "anything goes" type of society these days, there are still some women who do not want to be a married man's mistress. Tie up any lose ends--it will help you start the next chapter in your life with one less hindrance.

Moving Forward

As the next chapter in your life is ready to begin, the Cue Cards that follow will help you start off on the right path.

Cue Card: To help heal, give yourself the gift of time.

One of the best things you can do for yourself is to take enough time to heal emotionally after a divorce. Spend time alone, learn to cook, hang out with friends, and perhaps take a trip to a place you've always wanted to visit. Most important, go slow and give yourself time to feel better emotionally. Regardless of how bad your marriage was, divorce is still a loss and, in addition to feelings of loss, many men struggle with feelings of failure. The good news is that in time these feelings will begin to subside and you will start to feel like your old self again. Be gentle with yourself and take as much time as you need to feel better—it will be the best way to make sure you're ready for a new relationship when the time is right.

Cue Card: It's okay to date, just be smart about it, and don't get seriously involved with someone for at least a year.

Even if your marriage wasn't great at the end, you may find yourself feeling lonely from time-to-time. If this describes you, you may want to consider stepping back into the world of dating. If you meet someone who interests you, don't be afraid to ask her out. A casual date for coffee to see if you're compatible is usually a safe bet, and if you find that you've enjoyed your time together, you can go out to the movies or to dinner for your next date. Take it slow and don't make the common mistake some men make when they meet someone post-divorce: don't get serious too fast. You will still ride a rollercoaster of emotions for some time after your divorce, and it's not really fair to you or the woman you enter into a relationship with to pursue anything deeper until you've had enough time to fully process your feelings. You may long for companionship, but you can have that without moving in together by simply spending more time with one another if that's what feels comfortable for you. Also, dating a person for a year as I mentioned in Chapter Three is just a good rule of thumb anyway. In twelve months both of you will pretty much be able to see each other's highs and lows and determine if both of you are interested in taking your relationship to the next level.

Cue Card: Let your date know you've been married before, but don't go into too much detail until you've dated a while.

Hiding the fact that you've been married before isn't a piece of information you should "save for date three." Be upfront about your marital history--even if you've been married five times. The woman you date should have some idea of your relationship history because it will help her make a decision about whether or not she would like to continue seeing you. If she asks questions about your relationships, answer truthfully without getting into too many details or badmouthing your ex. After you've dated for a while, you may decide to share additional information, but going into everything that led to the demise of your previous marriage is too much to go into when you're just dating casually. The idea of initially dating someone is to have a light-hearted and fun time as you get to know one another. Deep talks about the problems in your previous relationship are usually best left out of your conversations for at least a couple of months until you know each other a little better.

Cue Card: Be selective and sensitive in who you decide to introduce to your children.

Of course, you would love your kids to accept the new partner you've decided to build a life with, but keep in mind that a large part of how they respond to and accept her will be determined by *how* you introduce her. If your children are younger, it's usually not a good idea to introduce them to any girlfriends you may have until you've met the one that you plan on getting serious with. Young children will have their own emotional issues tied to your divorce, and one of these issues will be a feeling of divided loyalty—introducing your children to a number of different girlfriends won't help them with that feeling in any way. (In addition, if your ex-wife sees that your actions are making your children upset, she may try to take you back to court for a different custody agreement.)

The relationship you share with your ex-wife can actually be a huge help in role modeling acceptance of a new member into your family. This is one of the reasons it's good to keep things civil and respectful with your ex-wife and come to an agreement on how you will handle your mutual love interests post-divorce. It's not uncommon for children of almost any age to want to take care of and come to the defense of a parent who is hurting. If you and your ex can come to amicable terms about how to handle the serious relationships the two of you have, your children will never have to feel that they have to "take sides" to help soothe the feelings of the parent they perceive as hurt. In turn, this will usually make your children more accepting of newcomers into the family system. If you're on good terms with your ex, you could schedule a family barbecue, invite your ex, her new boyfriend (if she has one), and your children—this will help take some of the awkwardness out of the situation because your children will be able to see that you and your ex are on good terms and happy for one another. If your relationship with your ex is strained, it is still important to inform her that you plan to introduce your new partner to your children so your ex is aware in the event the children ask her questions about it when they return to her. It's usually best to keep the first introduction casual and simple--go to the movies or go to an amusement park—do something that is light-hearted and fun so it's a positive first impression. Don't take it hard if your children aren't immediately accepting of your new partner despite your best efforts. The truth of the matter is that some children never fully accept a new partner in their biological parent's life.

When this is the case, aim for a civil and respectful relationship rather than trying to force a close relationship because all that will do is build anger and resentment for all individuals involved.

Cue Card: When you find a new partner and decide you would like to marry again, discuss how both of you will handle discipline with your children from your previous marriage.

One of the most difficult transitions in a step-parent/child relationship is how to discipline children. Don't leave it for your partner and children to figure out hoping "they'll find their balance," because they won't. Ideally, you, your new partner and your ex-wife will be able to sit down together to discuss how discipline and co-parenting issues will be handled. This way all of you will be on the same page, the discipline your children will receive will be consistent, all of you will be able to back one another up, and your children will not be able to pit one of you against the other which is very common in step-parent/blended family situations. Discuss household rules, school and homework expectations, chores, and what types of discipline will be implemented and under what circumstances. If you have a distant relationship with your ex, have this type of conversation with your new partner—this way at least the two of you will be on the same page.

A Closing Note

While you may try to be your best in all aspects of your life, sometimes things may not go as you had hoped because life will inevitably throw you a few curveballs. By using the skills you've read about in this book, you should be able to avoid many of the common relationship and life mistakes most men make. Remember, you are not only responsible for *your actions*, but you are also responsible for *your reactions*. As long as are being the best man that you can possibly be, that's really all you can do because you will never be able to control the responses and actions of others. When we bring our best self to any situation, we will usually have a better outcome and, most of the time, life should go the way we would like it to. If it doesn't though (and sometimes *it just doesn't*), don't beat yourself up—use it as an experience to learn and grow. If you've had a few failed relationships, try hard not to let your heart turn to stone. There is still much goodness out there. Stay positive, have hope that you will find someone, and in the meantime continue being your best—you have nothing to lose and everything to gain. Every day you are alive is a gift. Make the most of it.

ABOUT
KHARIS PUBLISHING

KHARIS PUBLISHING is an independent, traditional publishing house with a core mission to publish impactful books, and channel proceeds into establishing mini-libraries or resource centers for orphanages in developing countries. Every time you purchase a book from Kharis Publishing or partner as an author, you are helping give these kids an amazing opportunity to read, dream, and grow. Kharis Publishing is an imprint of Kharis Media LLC. Learn more at
https://www.kharispublishing.com.

Resources

Therapist Search Websites
American Association of Marriage and Family Therapists
www.therapistlocator.net

American Psychological Association
http://locator.apa.org

The National Board for Certified Counselors
www.nbcc.org/counselorfind

National Social Worker Finder
www.helppro.com/NASW/Default.aspx

ONLINE THERAPY

Better Help e-Counseling
www.betterhelp.com

Talkspace
www.talkspace.com

SUICIDE PREVENTION

National Suicide Prevention Lifeline
800-273-8255
www.suicidepreventionlifeline.org

DOMESTIC VIOLENCE RESOURCES

Center for Prevention of Abuse
800-559-SAFE (7233)
www.centerforpreventionofabuse.org

National Domestic Violence Hotline
800-799-SAFE (7233)
www.thehotline.org

PARENTING SUPPORT

www.fatherly.com

DIVORCE SUPPORT

MenLiving
www.menliving.org/divorce

Mensgroup
www.mensgroup.com

SUBSTANCE ABUSE SUPPORT

Substance Abuse and Mental Health Services Administration
800-662-HELP (4357)

CPSIA information can be obtained
at www.ICGtesting.com
Printed in the USA
LVHW020005081121
702717LV00006B/69

9 781637 460771